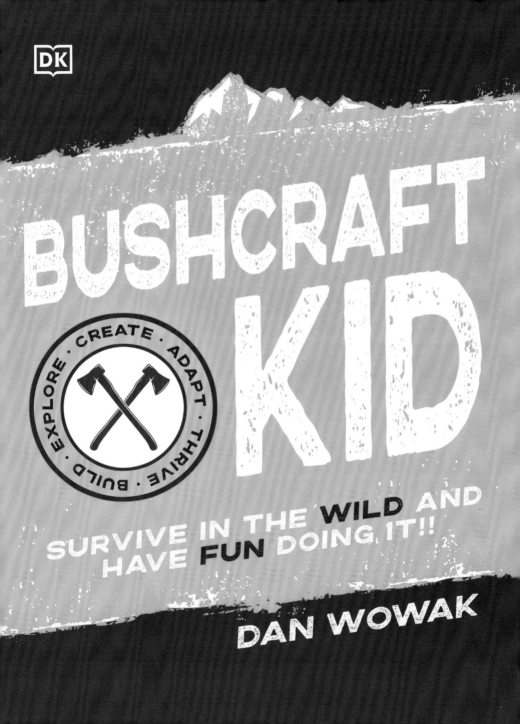

BUSHCRAFT KID

EXPLORE · CREATE · ADAPT · THRIVE · BUILD

SURVIVE IN THE WILD AND HAVE FUN DOING IT!!

DAN WOWAK

Publisher Mike Sanders
Senior Editor Brook Farling
Art & Design Director William Thomas
Assistant Director of Art & Design Rebecca
Batchelor
Proofreader Lisa Starnes
Indexer Brad Herriman

First American Edition, 2022
Published in the United States by DK Publishing
1745 Broadway, 20th Floor, New York NY 10019

Copyright © 2022 by Dan Wowak
23 24 25 10 9 8 7 6 5 4
005-327661-APR2022

Published in the United States by Dorling Kindersley
Limited

A catalog record for this book
is available from the Library of Congress.
ISBN 978-0-74405-383-8
Library of Congress Catalog Number: 2021944037

DK books are available at special discounts when
purchased in bulk for sales promotions, premiums,
fund-raising, or educational use. For details, contact:
SpecialSales@dk.com

Printed and bound in China

All images © Dan Wowak
For further information see: www.dkimages.com

For the curious
www.dk.com

MIX
Paper | Supporting
responsible forestry
FSC™ C018179
FSC
www.fsc.org

This book was made with Forest
Stewardship Council ™ certified
paper - one small step in DK's
commitment to a sustainable future.
For more information go to
www.dk.com/our-green-pledge

CONTENTS

INTRODUCTION

When I was a kid, an early dismissal from school because of a snowstorm was always welcomed. I remember rushing home to pack my outdoor gear so I could head into the woods. With snow falling and my backpack loaded, I would climb the mountains that surrounded my town. Looking back, I can't tell you what the actual purpose was of doing that, but I can tell you it was always an adventure. Being in the woods was a staple in my life from when I was a young boy. Fishing with my grandparents, camping with friends, and even hiking during those snowstorms in the Appalachians molded me into the woodsman I am today. From as early as I can remember, I was interested in being outside. And I was also always excited about the gear I carried. I would pack, unpack, and repack my gear. And it was just as fun as actually being out in the woods.

Back in those days, I never knew of, or had even heard of, bushcraft; I just knew that when I went into the woods, it was going to be a challenge. (And I can tell you that even after 30 years, it's still a challenge and that will never change, but that's also what makes it fun.) The weather, the terrain, even the time of day all presented unique situations. I soon realized that with just my gear and the knowledge I possessed, I could make Mother Nature work in my favor. I could use what nature provided to beat the elements and make life better in the woods, so that's what I did. I ditched all the high-tech gadgets and went old school. I would think about what men on the frontier carried or what my grandfather carried when he went camping. I researched how both men and women who lived remotely would thrive. Soon I was carrying heavy-duty canvas backpacks, wool blankets, and most importantly, tools like a belt knife, an axe, a flint and steel kit, and ropes to all help make camp life better.

As I've spent time outside over the years, I've made my camps a home away from home. I've built hooks to hang my gear, benches to sit on, and work tables to help me carve things. I've cooked delicious meals and made them with cooking tools I created simply, with materials I found in the forest around me. Soon I realized that nearly every comfort I had at home I could have in the woods. What's interesting is that even back when I didn't know about bushcraft, it's what I was doing every time I went outside. It wasn't until I got a bit older that I started to hear about bushcraft. And although I can't remember the first time I heard the term, I started to realize that bushcraft was what I had been doing all along and it's the thing I love to do in the woods. And what's best about it is that anyone can do it. It's customizable to what you like to do; there are no rules! Bushcraft is simply about having fun in the woods with your gear and with nature around you.

Spending time in the woods brings happiness and a sense of accomplishment to everyone, and I wrote this book because I want you to get outside and enjoy the outdoors. I outline many of the essential skills you should learn when you're heading into the outdoors. But don't worry if you've never done any of it before! Learning bushcraft skills takes time, and as you go on more and more outdoor adventures, you'll incorporate more and more of these skills. We will cover everything from getting a good night's sleep, to starting a fantastic campfire, to making your own cooking utensils. One of my favorite sayings is *another tool for the toolbox*. I want you to try to think of all of the skills you're about to learn as tools for your bushcraft toolbox. And just like with normal tools at a shop, you won't use them all at once, but as problems arise. If you forget a drinking cup, you'll know how to make one with birch bark! If you have wet boots, you'll learn how to make a boot dryer! We will talk about all of that and tons more.

Bushcraft is my life and has been my life since a young boy. I hope you find as much excitement and relaxation with it as I have over my life. And I hope you find bushcraft to be as fun as I did as a kid, and it gets you excited to get into the woods. Enjoy!

–Dan Wowak

1

PREPARING FOR YOUR OUTDOOR ADVENTURE

Planning your outdoor trip can be just as fun and exciting as the adventure itself. Looking at maps, finding out what the weather will be like, and packing your gear are all exciting parts of planning an outdoor adventure. In this chapter, we will take a look at some important things to consider when planning an awesome outdoor adventure, and you'll learn how to pack smart!

WHAT IS BUSHCRAFT?

Bushcraft is the art of creating useful solutions to solve problems in the outdoors. It's about more than just learning survival skills—it's about using tools and mostly just the materials that nature provides to create solutions. Yes, you always need to carry some gear as you embark on any adventure, but you can't carry everything, so why not learn how to make some of the things you'll need while you're out there? It doesn't matter if you'll be spending just a few hours outside or if you're going on a multi-day trip, bushcraft will fuel your adventure and add to the fun!

YOU'LL BE A PROBLEM SOLVER AND A BUILDER

Think about this: If a bridge needs to be built, engineers begin the process by figuring out how to build the bridge. They'll use tools like calculators and computers to develop blueprints and figure out the best way to build the bridge. Next, construction workers will gather all of the necessary materials for the project and get to work: pouring concrete, setting metal beams, and laying asphalt. Before long, the bridge is completed and a problem that was there before has now been solved: the bridge provides an easier way for people to drive their cars from one point to another. Much like a construction company designs and builds a bridge, bushcrafters design solutions to solve problems by using materials and tools to make something that is needed and useful. When bushcrafters have problems to solve, they are the engineer and the construction worker, but they're also the driver who ultimately uses the bridge because they use the solution they've created to make outdoor life a little easier and a little more enjoyable. A bushcrafter sees a need, designs a solution, builds the solution, and then uses the solution.

The most exciting part of bushcrafting is that other than staying safe, there really are no rules! If you can dream up a solution, create it, and put it to use, it's a success!

BUSHCRAFT IS MORE THAN JUST CAMPING

Bushcraft is about making camp life comfortable—making your camp a home away from home, but without hauling tons of gear into camp to make it happen. Of course, you're going to learn camping basics like how to build campfires and set up shelters, but you'll also learn how to tie useful knots, carve handy tools, build unique cooking setups, and sleep comfortably in the outdoors. (You'll even learn how to make a surprisingly comfortable "mattress" out of just debris and logs.) Most importantly, you're going to learn how to make all kinds of cool things, which is what bushcraft is really about. You'll learn how to carve hooks to hang your clothes on, how to make cooking tools, how to make your own fire extenders as well as things like a boot dryer, a birch basket, pine glue, and more. You'll even learn how to make a comfy camp toilet!

PLANNING YOUR TRIP

One of the most exciting parts of any outdoor adventure is the planning stage. Here are some tips for choosing a destination and planning your outdoor adventure.

CHOOSING A DESTINATION

There are so many cool outdoor places to explore and visit! State and national parks and forests can provide some great areas to enjoy outdoor activities, including designated hiking and camping areas, and these places have lots of information online that will explain everything the locations have to offer, but they can also have some limitations. Many of these locations have pretty strict rules and regulations that limit camping to designated areas and don't allow the cutting of trees or branches, which often are used for bushcrafting projects. If you choose to camp in a designated campground or park, be sure to read up on what is allowed and what is forbidden.

For bushcrafting, private or undesignated public land is often a better option. Talk to friends or family who own private land to see if they will allow you to access the land for your adventure. If they do grant permission to use their property, you'll have much more freedom when making your camp—just remember to be a good steward of the land, be cautious with fire, and leave no trace that you were there. If you can't get access to private land, you can still practice many bushcraft skills at home. Most bushcraft skills can be practiced almost anywhere.

EVALUATING YOUR NEEDS

Wherever you decide to go, it's important to evaluate your needs before you pack your gear. Here are some important questions to consider before you pack up and hit the road:

- **What will the conditions be like?** Will it be a forest where there are lots of insects? Or are you heading into the mountains where it could be cold? Will it be a desert environment where water is scarce and you'll be dealing with temperature extremes?

- **How long will you be gone?** The length of your trip will determine which supplies you'll need to take and how much of those supplies you'll need to bring along. (Food, in particular, is an important one to consider.)

- **What time of year is it?** What are all the possible weather scenarios you might encounter? This will help you decide what kind of clothing you will need to take, in addition to what kind of shelter supplies you will need to pack.

Thinking about these factors before you pack your gear is an important step in the planning stage. It will help you decide what to take and what to leave at home.

LEARNING ABOUT YOUR LOCATION

Before leaving for your trip, you'll want to research the location where you'll be camping to ensure you pack the right tools and supplies, and will be prepared for whatever you'll encounter.

LEARN ABOUT THE ANIMALS, BUGS, SNAKES, AND PLANTS

It's helpful to know what living things will be in the area where you'll be setting up camp. Many people avoid spending time outdoors because they are afraid that animals are going to come after them or bugs are going to bite them. This is really unfortunate because this is very uncommon; most creatures are harmless, and a lot of them are more afraid of you than you are of them. More often than not, those creatures will add to the fun of your adventure and will give you something to seek out and explore. As you prepare for your trip, do some research and find out if there are any animals in the area you should avoid and also if there are interesting animals you might be able to spot. Are there any bugs or snakes you should keep an eye out for?

Are there any toxic plants like poison ivy or poison oak? Are there plants that might supply you with food or materials you'll need for projects? These are the kinds of questions you'll want to consider as you prepare.

CHECK THE WEATHER

It's important to know about the weather when camping. Understanding that it gets cold in the winter is important because when you start packing for the trip, you'll want to pack lots of warm clothes and dress in layers. (Wearing flip flops in the snow wouldn't be a good idea!) Packing for a summer trip, on the other hand, means you'll need fewer clothes, but it will require a completely different set of gear that will help you deal with insects and heat. Your priorities for a winter trip likely will be staying warm and nourished, while your priorities for a summer trip will be keeping cool and dry. Staying hydrated will be critical on all types of trips.

RESEARCH THE LAND FEATURES

Any location you decide to go to will have unique land features. Hanging out near a lake for a weekend will be very different than being in the desert for a weekend. Will you need to pack extra water because there will be a scarcity of fresh water? Will you need to pack supplies that will provide sufficient shelter from the hot sun? Is it hot during the day but cool at night? Are there plenty of natural materials for making your projects, or are materials scarce? Understanding what is plentiful in the area and what is scarce will help make both packing and the trip itself more enjoyable.

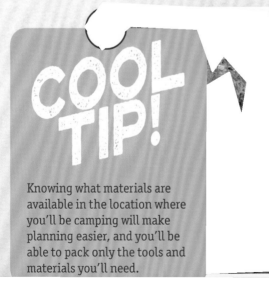

COOL TIP!

Knowing what materials are available in the location where you'll be camping will make planning easier, and you'll be able to pack only the tools and materials you'll need.

DETERMINING YOUR SURVIVAL PRIORITIES

Every outdoor experience requires the same things we have at home . . . well, sorta! We need a place to sleep, food to eat, and water to drink, as well as the means to stay warm, cook our food, and use the toilet. These important things are called *survival priorities,* and they include shelter, food, water, and fire, as well as any tools and supplies we'll need in order to survive and build the things we'll need while we're out there.

When you go on an outside adventure, it's important to bring along all the tools and supplies you'll need to fulfill your needs. Now that you've researched your location and have a clear picture of what you might want to bring along, you need to determine exactly what you'll need to pack. Begin this process by writing down each of your survival priorities on separate pieces of paper and then listing exactly what you'll need to bring to fulfill your needs in each category. Once you've completed your lists, you can begin packing your gear.

FIRE

Fire provides heat to keep you warm, a means to cook your food, and also a way to boil and disinfect water. Fire can also help with some outdoor projects, such as making pine glue or searing the end of a rope so it won't unravel. You'll learn how to make a good campfire and use it properly.

WATER

No matter where your adventures take you, water is critical and you'll need to drink plenty of it in order to stay safe. Water helps our bodies function properly, allows our brains to work better, helps us cook our food, and helps us stay clean. Without water, you can become sick or dehydrated, so you'll learn how to gather and disinfect water for your camp.

SHELTER

We need to sleep when we're outdoors, and we also need to stay warm and dry. Shelter is essential, but it's easier than you think to build a shelter in the woods; all you really need is a tarp, rope to hold up the tarp, some stakes (which you'll make), and some bushcrafter know-how. There are different types of shelters, and some work better than others, depending on the situation, but you'll learn how to make several types.

FOOD

Food gives us the fuel we need to make it through the day. And besides, being hungry is no fun! Almost anything you can cook at home can be cooked in the outdoors. But if you want to keep things simple, snacks are an easy way to stay nourished. Look for snacks that don't need to be refrigerated or cooked. If you do want to cook, you'll need to plan ahead to keep ingredients safe prior to cooking. You might also need to take a cooler in warmer climates, while in colder climates there may be snow on the ground that you can use to keep your food cold. There are also freeze-dried meals you can pack that will only require adding water. Whatever you decide, you'll learn how to cook and enjoy meals at camp.

TOOLS AND SUPPLIES

Packing your tools is the most fun part of planning! The tools you'll carry will help you make everything better at camp. Before you pack your tools, think about any situations you will encounter and then add the necessary tools to your list that will fix those problems. What will you need to fix a broken backpack strap? What will you need to cut wood? Ask yourself these questions as you decide what to pack.

PACKING YOUR GEAR

Getting your gear ready for a trip is always fun—deciding what to bring, what not to bring, what you *want* to bring (but don't really need) is all part of the excitement of an outdoor adventure. So, now that you've researched your location and determined your survival priorities, it's time to figure out what to pack.

CHOOSING WHAT TO PACK

There are lots of different gear options to choose from, and you won't need to pack everything listed here. Once you've researched your location and determined your survival priorities, you can decide which items to pack.

Fire

What to Pack:
ferrocerium (ferro) rod; waterproof camping matches; flint and steel kit; homemade fire extenders like clothes dryer lint and duct tape

Water

What to Pack:
insulated water bottle (with carabiner) for carrying drinking water; portable water filter (pump, press, or straw models will all work); single wall, uninsulated metal water bottle for heating and sterilizing water in the campfire (this one is important)

Food

What to Pack:
shelf-stable snacks like trail mix, granola bars, beef jerky, or fruit roll-ups; instant oatmeal; freeze-dried food packs; ingredients for simple meals like spaghetti or grilled cheese sandwiches; drink mixes (for when you get tired of water)

Shelter

What to Pack:
8' x 8' (2.5m x 2.5m) square tarp; 30 feet (9m) of cotton clothesline rope; sleeping bag or wool blanket (depending on the weather); pillowcase that can be stuffed with grass or clothes to make a pillow

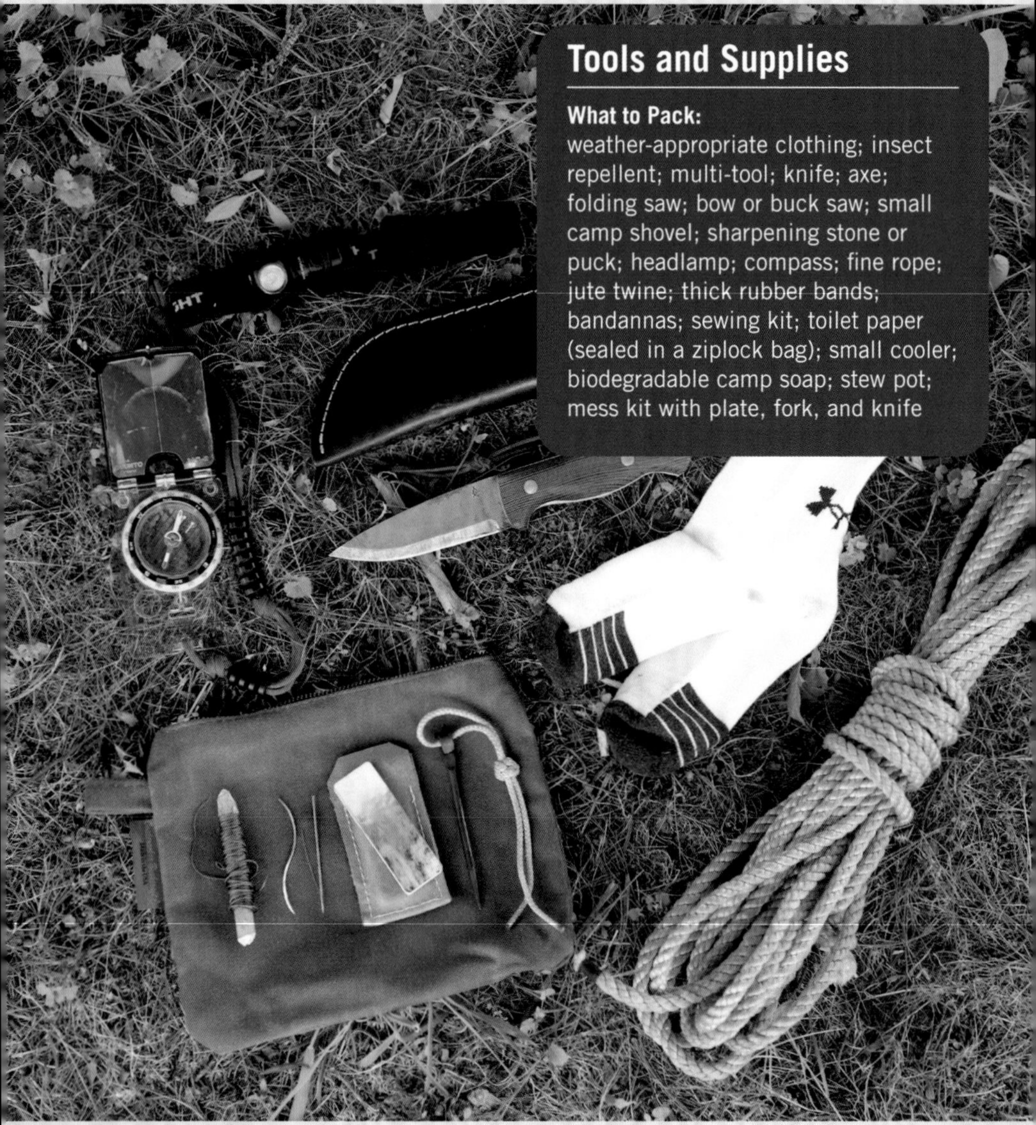

Tools and Supplies

What to Pack:
weather-appropriate clothing; insect repellent; multi-tool; knife; axe; folding saw; bow or buck saw; small camp shovel; sharpening stone or puck; headlamp; compass; fine rope; jute twine; thick rubber bands; bandannas; sewing kit; toilet paper (sealed in a ziplock bag); small cooler; biodegradable camp soap; stew pot; mess kit with plate, fork, and knife

TIPS FOR PACKING A BACKPACK

Here are some good guidelines for packing your gear properly.

- If you can't fit everything into your backpack, you'll need to decide what is essential and what can be left behind. Think about your essential needs first (building campfires, staying warm, staying hydrated, staying nourished), and leave behind anything else that isn't essential. You'll need to be able to carry your backpack wherever you go, so try to keep it light!

- If you are going to be outside for just a few hours or even for the day, you won't need to bring everything you would need for an overnight adventure. Leave sleeping bags and other shelter supplies at home.

- As you begin packing, place larger items you won't need right away in the bottom of the pack.

- Only carry food you know you'll eat. Carrying excess food means it could spoil, and it also will take up precious space in your backpack.

2

USING CUTTING TOOLS

Cutting firewood, trimming rope, and even preparing dinner at camp all require sharp cutting tools. Knives, axes, and saws are all important tools that every bushcrafter relies on to help get jobs done while they're out in the wilderness. In this chapter, we will discuss how to properly and safely use a knife, axe, and saw.

STAYING SAFE WITH CUTTING TOOLS

Cutting tools like knives, axes, and saws enable you to perform a variety of tasks around camp—from cutting sticks and branches to splitting firewood and preparing your food for dinner. Whatever the task, your cutting tools will likely play a role and will help get the job done, and they are also fun tools to use just so long as you use them safely. That's why it's always important to keep safety in mind when using your cutting tools—they can be extremely dangerous if used improperly. Keep in mind that if a tool can cut wood, it can easily cut you if you're not careful.

TWO SHAPES FOR SAFETY

When using any cutting tool around camp, it's important to remember two concepts for safety: the cutting circle and the danger triangle.

○ The Cutting Circle

The cutting circle, or blood circle, is the area around your body that, if someone is standing within, they can be injured. Before using your knife or axe, determine your cutting circle by standing up straight with one arm stretched out in front of you and then rotate your arm in a circle in front of your body. If your arm touches anyone or is even close to them, they are in your cutting circle and are at risk of being injured. If someone is in your cutting circle, it's *your* responsibility to move away from them to keep them safe.

The Cutting Circle The Danger Triangle

⚠ The Danger Triangle

The danger triangle, or triangle of death, is any area on your body that, if you cut yourself, it can be extremely dangerous. To find your danger triangle, stand up straight and then imagine a large triangle that extends from your chin down to your knees. Cutting yourself inside any area of this triangle can be extremely dangerous because inside this triangle are major arteries that transport blood from your heart to other parts of your body, including organs such as your liver and kidneys. If any of these areas are cut or punctured, it could be extremely serious and you would need to see a doctor immediately. Because of this, we always want to cut outside and away from the danger triangle.

THE PARTS OF A BUSHCRAFT KNIFE

There are lots of different types of knives, and they are all built a little differently, but these are the parts of the type of knife that is commonly used by bushcrafters while they're out in the wild. A good bushcraft knife needs to be sturdy, have a thick blade with a sharp edge, and be made of high-quality steel.

POINT The point is the very end of the knife blade and is used to puncture or pierce dense objects. This part of the knife is incredibly sharp, so you need to be extra careful around this part when you're handling your knife.

CUTTING EDGE The cutting edge is the sharp side of the blade. It's important to keep the cutting edge clean and extra sharp. And because this part of the knife is very sharp, you'll need to be extra careful around it when handling a knife.

SPINE The spine is the dull, flat, unsharpened edge on the top of the blade. You can use this side of the knife to apply pressure to the cutting edge.

HANDLE The handle is where you grip the knife. It also contains screws or rivets that attach the handle to the blade.

LANYARD HOLE The lanyard hole is simply the hole where the lanyard is threaded.

LANYARD The lanyard is a piece of rope or leather that is attached to the knife through the lanyard hole. The lanyard allows you to pull your knife from the sheath more easily, and it can also be worn around your wrist to keep the knife from flying out of your hand or dropping on your foot as you're using it.

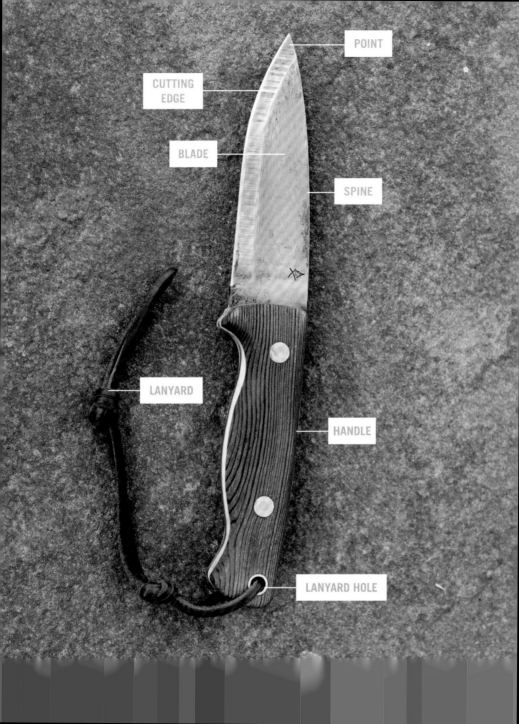

POINT

CUTTING EDGE

BLADE

SPINE

LANYARD

HANDLE

LANYARD HOLE

HOW TO USE A KNIFE

There are lots of different ways to use knife, but these are the safest methods and should always be used when you're cutting or carving anything with a knife.

EMPLOYING THE FIST GRIP

Before you cut anything, it's important to hold the knife correctly by using the fist grip. To employ the fist grip, grasp the knife with a full fist, with all your fingers wrapped around the handle and the sharp edge facing away from your body. This will give you the most power and control over the blade.

CUTTING USING THE CHEST-LEVER METHOD

To cut using the chest-lever method, grasp the handle with a fist grip with the blade reversed in your hand, as if the knife is being held backward. Place the handle end of the knife near the center of your chest and hold the piece of wood in the opposite hand. Using your back muscles, push the knife blade outward. (This is a good technique for smaller individuals who may not have the strength to cut using just their arm.)

CUTTING USING THE KNEE-LEVER METHOD

To cut using the knee-lever method, grasp the knife with a fist grip with the cutting edge facing forward. Rest your hand against your leg with the back of your hand facing up—only your hand should be touching your leg, not the knife. (This will give you a very secure grip and will keep the knife from moving.) While keeping your knife stationary, pull the piece of wood you want to cut back toward you and across the knife blade.

Move the knife away from your body

Pull the object toward you

THE PARTS
OF AN AXE

An axe is the ultimate bushcraft tool; it's robust and ready to get the job done. From small, fine cutting jobs to chopping firewood or cutting wood for projects, the axe can make it all happen.

HEAD The metal part of the axe. Axe heads come in a variety of shapes, sizes, and weights.

BIT The sharpened edge of the head; it's the part that does the cutting.

TOE The very top tip of the bit. This part is useful for carving or cutting small objects whenever you're using your axe more like a knife blade.

HEEL The lowest part of the bit. This is the most-used area of the blade: it's the first part to hit when you're chopping wood and the part used to line up the axe head when using the triangle method for splitting.

EYE The hole at the top of the axe head where the handle comes through the head.

POLL The flat edge on the back of the axe head. It can be used like a hammer, but only on wood. (You should never pound metal nails or metal tent pegs with the back of your axe, as they could damage it.)

CHEEK The metal area on the head behind the sharp cutting edge. Axe cheeks can be thick or thin, depending on the axe. Axes with thinner cheeks are great for carving, while axes with thicker cheeks are great for splitting wood.

HANDLE The wooden part you hold to control the axe. Axe handles come in a variety of lengths and shapes, and can be made from a variety of materials.

KNOB The flat end of the axe handle.

LANYARD EYE A hole at the end of the axe handle that holds a lanyard. (When storing an axe, it's best to lay it flat or hang it from a lanyard. Leaning it against a wall can warp the handle over time.)

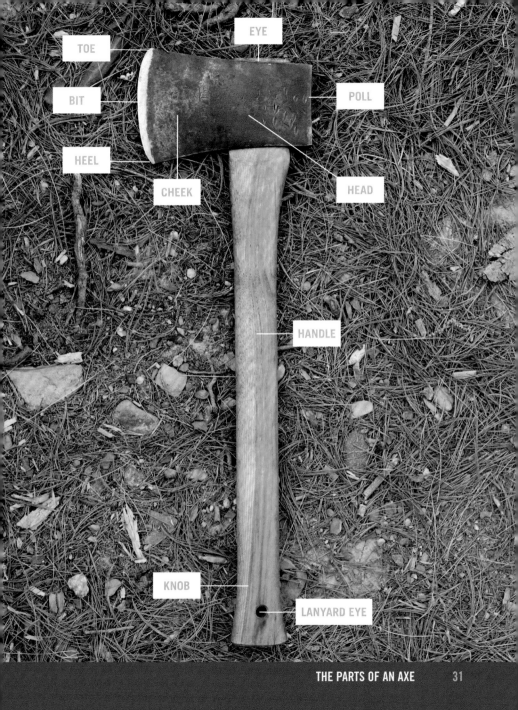

TOE

EYE

BIT

POLL

HEEL

CHEEK

HEAD

HANDLE

KNOB

LANYARD EYE

HOW TO USE AN AXE

Using an axe can be just as dangerous, if not more so, than using a knife, so it is important to use it properly. Here are some tips that will help you use this handy tool safely and effectively.

FINDING THE RIGHT FIT

Axes come in all different shapes and sizes, and choosing one can be confusing. A bushcraft axe should never be longer than 23 inches (58cm); larger axes are meant for splitting large wood or chopping down large trees, which isn't something a bushcrafter needs to do. To keep it simple, don't buy an axe that has a handle longer than your arm. And try to pick an axe with a head that is just slightly larger than your hand. This should be about the right weight for you, and you should be able to use it without getting too tired.

USING THE PROPER GRIP

It's important to grip an axe properly. If you're right-handed, you should place your left hand just above the base of the handle and then place your right hand above your left hand. This will allow you to hold the axe with your nondominant hand, but control the pressure of the axe with your dominant hand. (If you're left-handed, simply reverse the hand positions.) Hold the axe with a firm, but not overly tense grip.

Right-handed grip

USING A CUTTING ANVIL

Cutting into the air with a knife or an axe can result in you losing control of the tool after you make the cut, which can be very unsafe. Cutting into a tree stump, a downed log, an exposed root, or a standing tree will help keep you safe. In the woods, we call this type of cutting surface an *anvil*. Whether chopping with an axe or cutting with a knife, always try to use an anvil. When using an anvil, you'll be cutting just like you would on a cutting board at home. Also, you never want to cut onto rocks or dirt; they can both damage your axe blade.

Whenever you're splitting firewood with an axe, position yourself in a way that if you miss the wood or the axe bounces off the wood, the axe blade will hit the ground and not somewhere on your body. If you don't have a cutting stump or tree log to use as a cutting surface, kneel down and place the wood directly on the ground. If the axe misses the target, the next thing in the path of the axe will be the ground, and not your foot or leg. It's always better to have a chipped axe bit than a missing toe!

USING THE TRIANGLE METHOD TO CUT FIREWOOD

When most people typically think of splitting firewood at camp, they think of creating large, neatly stacked piles of wood. Bushcrafters, however, have to pick and split their own wood, so chopping large pieces is usually too difficult of a task. Smaller pieces about the diameter of your arm are actually perfect for campfires. These pieces sometimes still need to be split, though, and that's when you can use the *triangle method* for splitting your firewood. To use the triangle method, position your axe bit (the sharp edge of the head) in the center and toward the top end of the wood. Next, position the knob (the end of the handle) on the opposite end of the wood you're trying to split so that the axe handle and head are both now resting on the wood. This will create a triangle between the axe and the wood. Wrap both hands around the wood and axe handle at the point where the knob meets the wood. Lift the wood and axe upward as one piece, and then strike downward with force on a cutting stump or a fallen tree log to split the wood. This eliminates the need to swing your axe and will keep you and everyone around you safe.

Axes are not just made for swinging! An axe is a great replacement for a knife. Simply choke up, or move your hand up the axe handle, to the head of the axe. This will give you more control of the axe head and allow you to cut with more precision.

USING SAWS

Saws give you the ability to cut lots of wood quickly and with little effort. They can provide straight, smooth cuts on small pieces of wood, which can be extremely useful for creating different bushcraft projects, or they can be used for cutting large pieces of firewood for splitting. There are different types of saws that can be used in the outdoors, and they all look slightly different and offer different advantages and disadvantages.

CHOOSING A SAW

There are three main types of camp saws: *folding, bow,* and *buck.* A *folding saw* is easy to handle and can fit into tight spaces, making it ideal for cutting small saplings and branches, but it's typically too small for cutting large pieces of wood. A folding saw is compact and won't add a lot of weight to your pack, making it easy to carry into camp, but because it has a small blade, it will require a lot of effort to cut large logs. A *bow saw* is big and bulky, but it will enable you to quickly cut larger pieces of wood with ease. However, because a bow saw is large and can't be disassembled, it really isn't convenient to carry if you're hiking into camp on foot. A *buck saw* is large like a bow saw and also will enable you to process larger pieces of wood, but it can be broken down into pieces to make it slightly easier to pack and carry. (Just be very careful while handling the blade.)

When deciding what kind of saw to carry into woods, ask yourself what you're going to be using it for. Are you going to be cutting lots of large wood for campfires? If so, a bow saw or buck saw might be your best option, just so long as you're able to carry it into camp. If you're entering camp in a way other than by foot, such as in a canoe, you can usually still carry a larger saw with ease. If you're only going to be cutting small branches and saplings, a smaller folding saw is likely the best option, and you'll be able to carry it in your pack or even in your pocket.

FOLDING
SAW

BOW
SAW

BUCK
SAW

SAW BLADES

Just like there is more than one type of saw, there are different types of saw blades. Dry wood blades will cut live wood (green wood) more slowly than green wood blades, but they will make smoother, more precise cuts, which is why most bushcrafters prefer using them over green wood blades. Green wood blades won't cut green wood with the same level of precision as dry wood blades, but they have something called *rakers* mixed in with the teeth, and these rakers help clear out the wet green wood shavings as you saw, so they can cut green wood a little more efficiently than dry wood blades, but just not as cleanly.

DRY WOOD BLADE

GREEN WOOD BLADE

USING A SAW

Using a saw is simple. Place the piece of wood you want to cut on a stable surface, and hold it with your free hand placed as far from the saw blade as possible, but still close enough to hold the wood securely. Firmly grasp the saw and place the blade of the saw onto the wood. Begin by drawing the saw back toward you to start the cut, and then push it away from you. Repeat the action, slowly and steadily, while letting the saw blade do the work. You should always avoid forcing the blade or moving too quickly, which can cause the blade to get stuck or jump from the wood.

If you're sawing and your blade jumps off the wood, you've experienced what is called *blade jump*. Blade jump can be dangerous and usually happens when you push forward too hard while trying to make the saw cut too quickly. When the teeth of the saw blade can't cut the wood quickly enough to match the pressure being applied to the saw, the saw can fly up and away from the wood, possibly hitting your hand and causing injury. To prevent blade jump, take your time and allow the saw to do the cutting, instead of forcing it. There is no need to push excessively; a good, sharp saw will get the job done without the need for a lot of force.

FUN FACT!

Not all saws work the same. Some only cut on the pulling action, while others cut during both the pushing and pulling actions.

WHAT TO DO WHEN THE SAW BLADE GETS STUCK

When you cut wood with a saw, you are removing wood fibers and leaving a gap, or what is called a *kerf*. If your saw blade gets stuck in a piece of wood, it's likely because the saw is pinched in the kerf. The kerf will only be the thickness of the saw blade, and as you cut deeper into the wood, the gap above the saw isn't always supported and can sometimes close and pinch the saw blade. To avoid pinching the blade, make sure only one end of the piece you are cutting is supported so that the other end can fall away freely when the cut is completed. If both ends are supported, the weight of the two ends will likely push the pieces together and pinch the blade.

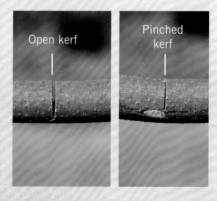

Open kerf

Pinched kerf

3

CREATING KNOTS AND LASHINGS

Bushcrafters don't use nails to hold wood pieces together; they rely on rope and knots to do the job. Knots can feel a little overwhelming when you're just starting to learn them, but fortunately bushcrafters only use a few. And the cool thing about these knots is they are really easy to learn and will help you make just about anything in the woods that requires rope! In this chapter, you will learn how to tie the most commonly used bushcraft knots and lashings.

KNOTS

TYING A SQUARE KNOT

This knot is useful for when you want to tie two ends of a single line together in order to bundle an object.

1 Wrap the rope around the object you want to bundle. Cross the ends of the rope, right end over left end.

2 Tuck the right end around and behind the left end.

Continue by bringing the right end back up and over the left end. (If needed, pull up additional line to ensure you have enough line on both ends to finish the knot.)

Cross the ends again, making sure the original right end once again crosses over top of the original left end.

Tuck the right end behind the left end and then back up and through the loop.

Pull both ends of the rope to cinch the knot tight.

KNOTS

TYING A BOWLINE KNOT

This knot is used to make a fixed loop in the end of a line.

1 Make a small loop approximately 12 inches (30.5cm) from the end of the rope.

2 Pull the end of the rope back and insert it under and then up through the first loop to create a second, larger loop to the right of the first loop. (This second loop is going to be the fixed loop at the end of the knot.)

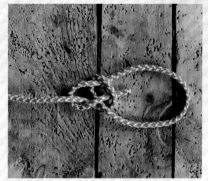

 Pull the end of the rope down and underneath the rope.

 Thread the end back through the original loop.

Holding the end of the rope with one hand and the long end of the rope with the other hand, cinch the knot tight to create the fixed loop.

FUN FACT!

Here's a fun little trick to help you remember how to tie a bowline knot: After you make your first loop, you call the cut end of the rope the "rabbit." Bushcrafters say the "rabbit" comes out of the hole (step 2), around the tree (step 3), and then back into the hole (step 4).

KNOTS

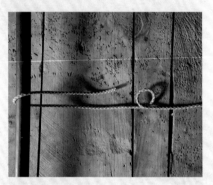

TYING A TRUCKER'S HITCH

This is a tensioning knot used to tie down items or to secure a tight line between two objects so you can set up things like tarp shelters between trees.

1 Tie one end of the rope to a stationary object, and then wrap the other end around the second object you want to tie it to. Next, create a small loop in the line.

2 Bunch the rope to the left of the loop to create a "hook."

3 Pull the "hook" through the loop by just a few inches.

 Grasp the rope on each side of the loop, and pull to cinch the knot tight.

 Pull on the rope to create tension on the line, and then thread the end of the rope through the newly created loop and then back over the newest large loop to create another small loop to the left of the original.

Thread the end of the rope up through the newest loop and then back down to create one more loop at the top.

Pull the end of the rope to cinch the knot tight.

KNOTS

TYING A PRUSIK KNOT

This is a friction hitch used to attach a loop of rope to another rope. It works great for hanging tarp shelters and is unique because if you push it at the wrappings, you can easily slide the loop along the larger line to make adjustments. However, if you grasp the loop itself and try to pull it along the larger line, it will not move because the three wraps create tension on the larger line and that tension helps keep the loop in place.

1 Place a knotted loop of small rope underneath the larger line you wish to tie it to.

2 Thread the knotted end of the loop over the larger line and then down through the looped end.

 Thread the knotted end up over the larger line again and then back down through itself again.

 Repeat the process until you've looped the smaller line through itself three times.

 Grasp the knotted end of the small rope, and pull down to cinch the knot tight. You can now secure a second rope inside the loop.

TYING A CLOVE HITCH

This simple knot is perfect for starting or finishing a sheer or diagonal lashing or for adding a toggle to a tripod for cooking.

1 Wrap the end of the rope in an "X" shape around the object you want to secure it to.

2 Insert the end of the rope into the top of the "X," and then pull it through the bottom to tighten the knot.

TYING A SLIP KNOT

This is a loop created on the end of a line that tightens down when pulled. It's a great knot for starting a lashing.

1 Cross the ends of the rope to create a loop.

2 Loop the end underneath the rope and then back up toward the center of the initial loop to create a second, smaller loop.

3 Thread the end of the rope under and then through the second, smaller loop.

4 Pull the end of the rope to cinch the knot tight.

 **LASHINGS**

CREATING A STRAIGHT LASHING

This lashing is used to keep one end of an object, such as another rope or a split stick, secure.

1 Create a fold in the rope, and then place the fold against the object you are lashing. Cross the long end of the rope over the object.

2 Begin wrapping the rope around the object and down toward the fold. Be sure to keep the rope tight as you wrap it around the object.

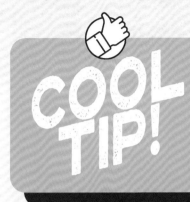

COOL TIP!

The straight lashing is frequently used to prevent sticks from splitting. If you are driving a tent peg into the ground and it begins to split, you can secure it with a straight lashing. You can also use a longer straight lashing to fix larger objects, like cracked tent poles.

 3 Once you're near the fold, thread the end of the rope into the newly created loop.

4 Pull the top end of the rope to make the loop disappear underneath the rope and cinch the lashing tight.

LASHINGS

CREATING A SHEER LASHING

This lashing is used to hold two or three sticks securely together.

 Begin by tying a slip knot around the sticks. Pull the rope tight.

 Wrap the rope around the sticks four or five times. Keep the rope tight as you wrap it around the sticks.

Wrap the rope between the sticks and around one stick twice.

4 Loop the end of the rope around the original wraps and between the sticks.

5 Insert the end of the line between the original wraps, and pull the end to tighten the lashing.

COOL TIP!

Don't forget that a sheer lashing can be used on either two or three sticks. This lashing is perfect for making a tripod for camp cooking or for suspending your gear off the ground in wet conditions.

 # LASHINGS

CREATING A DIAGONAL LASHING

This lashing is used to hold two sticks together when they meet in a crisscross fashion.

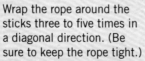 Cross the two sticks that are to be lashed together at 90 degrees. Create a slip knot over both of the sticks.

 Wrap the rope around the sticks three to five times in a diagonal direction. (Be sure to keep the rope tight.)

 Wrap the rope diagonally in the other direction three to five times.

4 Make sure the diagonal wraps are tight, and then wrap the rope around both lashings twice to tighten the diagonal lashes.

5 Finish the lashing by tucking the end under one of the wraps and pulling it to tighten the lashing.

COOL TIP!

Pulling a lashing tight as you tie it will help ensure that the lash will hold the sticks in place and not allow them to slide. Sometimes this can be tricky because these knots require a lot of movements and wraps, but don't get frustrated. The more you practice, the better at it you will get.

4

HONING YOUR SURVIVAL SKILLS

Bushcraft skills are super fun to learn and use, but before you head into the woods, it's important that you learn a few survival skills that can help keep you safe. In this chapter, we explore how to find and purify water, how to perform first aid on yourself and others, and how to use navigation skills to find your way out of the woods should you get lost. The skills in this chapter will help make your days and nights in the woods much more exciting and also much safer.

FINDING SAFE WATER SOURCES

It can be difficult to find water in some outdoor environments like deserts, but it's pretty easy to find water in most other outdoor environments like forests. Making that water safe for drinking and cooking, however, requires some effort. Once you've located a useable source, you'll need to first treat the water to ensure it's safe to use.

USING WATER FROM LAKES, STREAMS, AND PUDDLES

Keep these things in mind when using water from any ground source:

- **Always disinfect water from lakes, streams, or puddles.** Water typically comes from two sources: the ground (aquifers) or the sky (rain or snow). The water you might collect from lakes, streams, or puddles has likely come from multiple sources, and it's unlikely you'll be able to identify where the water in those ground sources came from. Because of this, the water could be contaminated and make you sick, so you should always disinfect the water through boiling. It's super important to disinfect water from any ground source before using it for anything, even bathing or washing your hands.

- **Know the difference between disinfecting and purifying.** Disinfecting water is the process of killing viruses and bacteria through boiling. Boiling water will disinfect water and make it safe to use, but it won't always remove odd smells or tastes. Purifying is the process of making water pure, clean, and odor-free through filtering. The ideal approach is to both disinfect water through boiling and then purify it through filtering, but disinfected water is still almost always safe to use, even if it isn't free of odd tastes or smells.

WHY DO YOU NEED TO DISINFECT WATER?

Unlike the water you drink at home, water in the outdoors can contain microscopic viruses, bacteria, and parasites that can make you sick. Even if water looks crystal clear, it doesn't means it's safe to drink. The three most common backcountry viruses and bacteria found in water are *giardia, cryptosporidium,* and *E. coli,* and these contaminants generally come from the feces (poop) of animals. Animals, just like people, need water to drink, and they often visit the same places for water as we do. And while they're there, they may go to the bathroom around those sources, causing the water to become unsafe to drink. There is also a chance an animal might die in or around a water source, and the decay of the animal can breed contaminants that are unsafe for us. For these reasons, it's very important to disinfect any water you drink from outdoor sources. This all might sound a little gross, but fortunately there are some simple steps you can take to make water completely safe to drink.

DISINFECTING WATER

Disinfecting water is very important: it ensures you'll have safe water for drinking and cooking. If you're using a tripod to cook, you can simply boil water in a large pot placed over a fire. However, if you're not using a tripod, you'll need to disinfect water in a metal water bottle placed directly into a campfire. This is a simple task, but removing the hot water bottle from the fire can be dangerous, so you'll need to use a toggle or a "Y" branch to safely remove the hot bottle from the fire.

DISINFECTING WATER IN A METAL WATER BOTTLE

1 Cut a small stick that is the diameter of your pinky finger and slightly longer than the opening of the water bottle. Cut a length of fine rope that is about 3 feet (1m) long.

2 Carve the ends of the stick so they're slightly rounded, and then cut a "V" notch on the stick that is slightly off center. Tie the rope onto the stick so that it's secured in the notch.

3 Fill an uninsulated, single-wall metal water bottle mostly full with water, and place it directly into the fire. (Don't put the cap on the bottle.) Allow the water to boil for at least three minutes, and then lower the toggle into the bottle until it catches the inside shoulder of the bottle. Lift the bottle up and out of the fire, and place it on a flat surface where it won't tip over. Once the water has cooled, carefully shift the rope to one side to remove the toggle from the bottle.

USING A "Y" BRANCH TO MOVE A HOT WATER BOTTLE

1 If you can't make a toggle to move the bottle, cut a long "Y" branch that is thin and flexible, and then carefully force the branch down into the bottle. The short side of the "Y" should flex inward while going through the mouth and then pop back open once inside the bottle.

2 Carefully lift the bottle out of the fire. Once the bottle is out of the fire, place the bottle on a flat surface where it won't tip over, and allow it to cool completely before removing the stick from the bottle.

FILTERING WATER

Once you've disinfected water through boiling, it will be safe to use for everything around camp, including cooking, bathing, drinking, and washing. However, disinfected water doesn't always taste or smell clean; sometimes disinfected water can be perfectly safe to use but still taste funny or contain odd smells. Because of this, filtering is an important, though not essential, step to take to make the water you use at camp taste and smell better.

USING STORE-BOUGHT FILTERS

Store-bought water filters provide a safe and easy way to filter and disinfect your drinking water when you're at camp. There are numerous styles of filters on the market, including press, pump, and straw models, and they all work in a similar fashion. Inside each filter are different layers of materials like activated charcoal, and each layer removes microscopic germs. The water becomes cleaner and more purified as it passes through each layer in the filter, removing tastes and smells and eventually making it safe to drink.

MAKING A THREE-TIER SYSTEM

Water from ground sources can often be very dirty and contain lots of sediment. Drinking this water is never a good idea; it can make you sick and also clog a store-bought filter, so it's important to filter out the sediment before boiling or filtering the water. A three-tier filter system can help with this and is made up of three levels of filtering, starting with coarse material like grass, followed by finer material like sand, and ending with very fine material like crushed charcoal. Each time you run water through the system, small particles will be removed, until you eventually have water that can be disinfected.

WHAT YOU NEED

3 long sticks of similar size and length

3 large squares of similar-sized, fine-mesh material or three bandannas

Fine rope or twine for lashing the sticks and the material

Filtering materials (grass, sand, crushed charcoal)

1 Make a tripod using three long sticks and fine rope. Use sheer lashings to connect the sticks at the top, and then splay the legs to form a tripod.

2 Lash three levels of fine-mesh material down the length of the tripod to create baskets.

3 In the top basket, add grasses (coarse); in the middle basket, add sand (fine); in the bottom basket, add crushed charcoal (very fine). Place a container on the ground directly below the tripod top to catch the water.

 Run the water through the system a few times to prime it and rinse the filtering materials.

5 Continue pouring the water through the filter until it runs clear. (At first, the water might appear dirtier than what you started with, but after a short time, it will begin to look clear.) Once the water runs clear, disinfect it in the campfire or filter it through a store-bought filter.

OTHER WAYS TO FIND AND FILTER WATER

There are some sources in nature that can filter water. And while nature doesn't work quite as efficiently as store-bought filters, these options can provide water that can then be disinfected.

TAPPING WATER VINES

Water vines are not always easy to find, but they can serve as a source of water. Look for large, thick vines that have smooth surfaces. To tap a water vine, use a folding saw to cut the vine. You should then see water drip out that you can capture and disinfect. Because the water has passed through dirt and tree roots, and eventually traveled into the vine, nature has done some filtering, and the water will be clear. Be sure to tap only smooth vines. Any fuzzy vines could be poison ivy!

DIGGING A COYOTE WELL

Dig a hole 1 to 2 feet (30cm to 60cm) away from the edge of a stream and deeper than the water level. Once the hole begins to fill with water, dig another 6 to 12 inches (16cm to 30cm). At first, the water in the hole will appear dirty, but left undisturbed it should clear up within an hour.

FUN FACT!

When you need water in the winter, ice is the most efficient choice. Snow is made up of about 80 percent air, while ice is made up of only about 5 percent air. Whatever you add to your pot will eventually turn to water, so snow will still work, but you'll need to work a lot harder to get the same amount of usable water from snow as you would from ice.

COLLECTING SNOW OR RAIN

You can use containers to capture rain or snow that falls from the sky and then use it for water. Rain or snow is water that was once on the ground, but has evaporated and collected in the sky as clouds, and has now fallen back down to earth. Unlike ground sources, this water is clean and safe to drink!

You can also collect snow and ice from the ground and use it as drinking water; however, if it's already melted or it's from sources that have touched the ground, you'll need to treat it the same as water collected from a puddle or a pond and disinfect it to ensure it's safe to drink.

WILDERNESS FIRST AID

TREATING BUG BITES, SCRAPES, AND CUTS

Bug Bites

There are lots of different bugs in the outdoors. Some like to fly around your head and land on your nose to drink your sweat; some like to crawl up your leg and say "hello." While this might all sound a little creepy, it's all just part of being outdoors, and the majority of insects are completely harmless. But there are a few that might bite or sting, causing itching or burning. If this happens, wash the area with cool, disinfected water, and add a cold compress (that's just a fancy name for a cold, wet towel) to the bite area. If there's a stinger stuck in your skin, ask an adult to help you remove it.

COOL TIP!

JEWELWEED — PLANTAIN

Jewelweed and plantain are both useful for calming itchy skin from things like poison ivy and bug bites. Simply rub the leaves on the affected areas, and the itching will stop!

Scrapes and Cuts

Scrapes and cuts can happen in a variety of ways and can range from very minor to extremely serious, but both are treated in similar ways.

For small cuts or scrapes:
Rinse the area with disinfected water, and remove any debris from the wound. Apply direct pressure with a piece of fabric for at least 10 minutes to stop the bleeding. Once the bleeding has stopped, apply a pressure dressing to the wound. (A pressure dressing can be something as simple as a clean bandanna that is firmly affixed over the wound.)

applying direct pressure

compression bandage

For more serious cuts that have pronounced bleeding:
Immediately apply a piece of fabric and apply direct pressure to the cut. Continue applying pressure for at least 10 minutes. (Don't keep checking the cut, as this will prevent the pressure from stopping the bleeding.)

For more serious cuts, apply a compression bandage to the area by placing a clean bandanna over the wound and then tying a second bandanna around the area to apply additional pressure and limit the bleeding. Seek professional medical attention immediately.

WILDERNESS FIRST AID

TREATING BURNS, SPRAINS, STRAINS, HYPOTHERMIA, AND HYPERTHERMIA

Sprains and Strains

It's easy and pretty common to twist an ankle or a knee when you're in the woods, or to fall and hurt a shoulder or wrist. The woods is a wild place and there are lots of rocks and roots that can get in the way when you're hiking through unfamiliar territory.

If you sprain or twist an ankle, and the ankle is already supported by your boot, you should leave the boot on your foot to support the ankle. Taking off the boot will remove the much-needed support for the injured area. If you're not wearing boots and need to add more support to the ankle, place short, sturdy sticks on each side of the ankle, and then tie off the sticks at both the top and bottom with first aid bandages, bandannas, or long pieces of fabric. If you fall and sprain your wrist, securely wrap the area with a dressing to support the injured area.

If you injure a shoulder, you can make a sling out of an extra T-shirt or bandanna. If you're wearing a tight shirt or coat, keep these items on; they will help support your injured shoulder. Keep the injured area elevated to prevent it from swelling.

Burns

One of the best things about being in the woods is sitting around a campfire, but not being careful around a campfire can be dangerous. Picking up a hot pan, touching a hot stick, or even sitting too close to the fire can all cause burns. The sun can even cause a burn if you don't cover up!

If you experience a burn, rinse the affected area with cool, disinfected water, and then use a small piece of fabric to gently clean away any debris in the burn area. Allow the area to air dry, and then lightly cover it with a clean dressing.

Hypothermia and Hyperthermia

Getting too cold or too hot can both be very dangerous situations in the outdoors. Getting too cold is called *hypothermia,* and it's a condition where your body can't warm up and stay warm enough to keep your heart and other vital organs safe. It can occur when you aren't dressed properly for cold temperatures or you somehow get wet while you're out in cold conditions. *Hyperthermia* is a condition where your body gets too hot and can't cool down to a safe temperature to protect your vital organs. It can occur when you're physically active in hot conditions. Both situations can be extremely serious and almost always require immediate medical attention, but there are some things you can do until help arrives.

What to do for hypothermia (too cold):

1. Light a campfire. You want to build as robust a fire as you can possibly build.

2. Immediately get out of any wet clothes and put on dry clothes. If you don't have dry clothes, wrap yourself in a blanket or sleeping bag.

3. Drink lots of warm fluids. (This will help warm your core.)

What to do for hyperthermia (too hot):

1. Immediately stop all physical activity, and rest for as long as is necessary.

2. Find a cool place that is out of the sun.

3. Drink cold fluids to help cool down your body's core.

4. If possible, sit in a cold stream, pond, or lake to further cool your body.

NAVIGATION BASICS

Navigating in the woods with a compass is an important skill for every bushcrafter to know. And while using a compass might seem a bit intimidating at first, once you understand how to use one and also understand some basic methods of navigation, you'll realize just how fun navigating in the woods can be.

CARDINAL DIRECTIONS

There are four cardinal directions: north, south, east, and west. As you learn how to use a compass, try to think of navigation like working in a circle or around a clock. A circle has 360 degrees, and north is at the very top and at 0 degrees, or 12 o'clock. As you turn a quarter turn clockwise to the right, you'll hit east, which is at 90 degrees on the circle, or 3 o'clock. Keep turning clockwise another quarter turn and you'll face south, which is at 180 degrees on the circle, or 6 o'clock. Make one more quarter turn and you will be facing west, which is at 270 degrees, or 9 o'clock. One more quarter turn brings you back to north and at 360 or 0 degrees on the circle (or 12 o'clock). If you can understand this concept, you've taken the first step to becoming a navigation expert!

TYPES OF NAVIGATION

There are several different ways to navigate in the wild. Compass navigation is the most common and most accurate, but nature also provides us with some ways to navigate through the woods.

Terrain Association

As you hike in and out of camp, always make mental notes of the features in the land that you pass as you walk. Did you cross a stream or a field? Was there a large patch of pine trees to your right when you came into camp? All of these things are small hints that nature will give you to help you find your way back to camp. Making note of them on the way out of camp will help get you back to camp safely.

The Sun

The sun provides another useful way to navigate in the outdoors. We all know that the sun always rises in the east and sets in the west. Right? So if you're at camp in the evening and you're watching the sun set, you'll know that direction is west when you get up the next morning. The sun will rise the next morning in the opposite direction, which will be east. You can then use the 360-degree-circle concept to easily identify all four of the cardinal directions.

Pace Counts

You can determine how far you've traveled by counting your paces (or steps). To count your paces, set up two sticks and try to roughly measure the distance between them. If the sticks are about 100 feet apart and it takes you 25 steps to go from one stick to the other, you'll know your approximate pace count for 100 feet is 25. You can use this pace count to measure the distance traveled by simply counting your steps as you walk. (It can be helpful to track the pace counts in a log book.)

USING A COMPASS

A compass is a lot easier to use than you might think. The red point on the needle in the center of the compass face will always be pointing north. And if the needle has two points, the red point will always be pointing north, while the black point will always be pointing south. As you turn to face different directions, the red needle point will always be pointing north, but the compass will tell you which direction you're facing.

HOW TO USE A COMPASS

Here's a simple way to practice using a compass.

1. Hold the compass out in front of you so you can still see the face. Make sure the compass is level and not tilted to any one side.

2. Turn to the direction you want to travel. Although the red point of the needle will continue pointing north, the compass will indicate on the *bezel* which cardinal direction you are facing. (The bezel is the part of the compass that has the cardinal directions and all the numbers on it.)

3. The bezel has a marking on it that looks like a little red house. This "red house" (also called the *doghouse* or *shed)* will also move as you turn the bezel. Using your free hand, slowly turn the bezel until the red house is aligned with the red point of the needle.

4. Once the red house and red needle point are aligned, the number at the top of the compass will indicate the direction and *bearing* in which you are facing and traveling. You can track your bearings in a log book to keep a record of all the directions you've traveled as you hike.

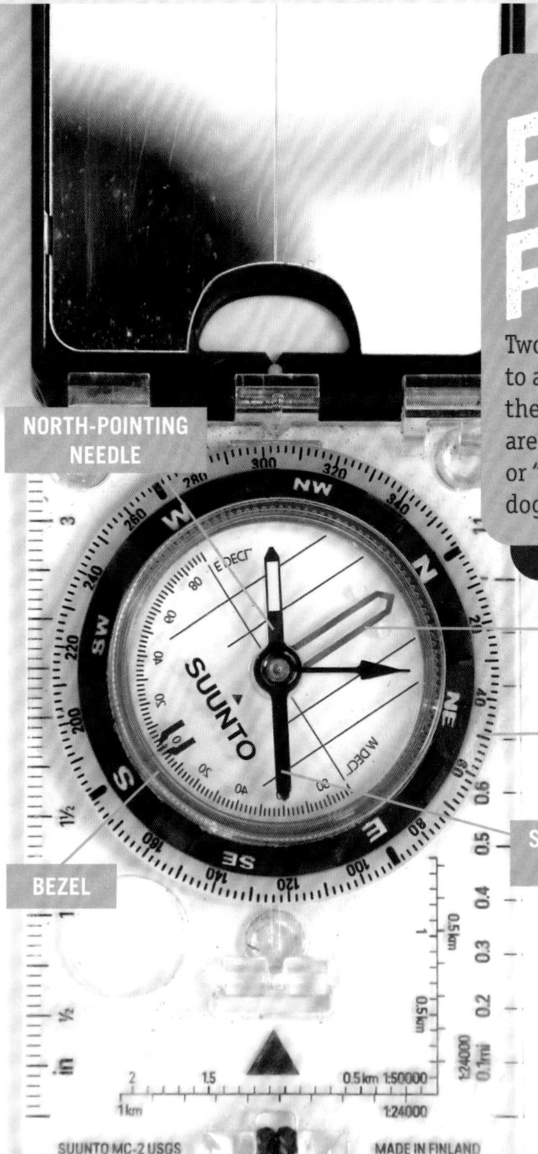

NORTH-POINTING NEEDLE
"RED HOUSE"
BEARINGS
SOUTH-POINTING NEEDLE
BEZEL
SUUNTO
SUUNTO MC-2 USGS
MADE IN FINLAND

FUN FACT!

Two easy ways to remember to align the red needle with the red house on the bezel are "put the red in the shed" or "put the needle in the doghouse"!

The red needle point is always pointing north, so this compass is facing north. Once the "red house" is aligned with the red needle point, this compass will show a bearing of 360 or 0 degrees.

NAVIGATION TECHNIQUES

Now that you've had a little practice with your compass, it's time to learn some navigation techniques that will put your compass to use. These methods can be used by bushcrafters as they begin navigation or when they might find themselves a little lost out in the wild. These techniques may seem a little challenging to master at first, but once you've practiced them a few times, you'll find out how fun it can be to use a compass.

In and Out Navigation

Here's a simple way to learn how to use your compass as you begin exploring in the woods.

1. Before walking into the woods, open your compass, hold it level, and face the direction you want to travel. The top of the compass will be facing the direction in which you will be traveling into the woods.

2. Adjust the bezel so the red needle is in the red house. (It's always a good idea to also write it down in a log book.)

3. Head into the woods and explore for a while. (Make sure you use terrain association and never wander off too far; you don't want to actually get lost.)

4. When you're ready to head back to camp, hold the compass level in front of you and begin turning your body until the black needle is in the red house. Once you do this, you will be pointed in the direction you need to walk to get back to camp. Remember: we always put our red needle in the red house (red in the shed) when we leave camp, so we need to remember to put the black needle in the red house (back is black) in order to return to camp in the opposite direction.

The Ray Method

If you've wandered off path and realize you are lost, you can use the ray method to find your way back to camp.

1. Wherever you are located, be it camp or a spot somewhere in the woods, consider it home for now. Don't worry, though, this won't be "home" for long!

2. Now, from "home," begin walking in any direction. (I know what you are thinking: Walk away from home and possibly get more lost? Yes, but trust me on this.) As you walk, blaze trees with whatever you might have available (pieces of fabric, charcoal, etc.). Be sure to mark *both sides* of each tree.

3. After you've walked for a while, simply turn around and follow your blazes back to "home" if you don't see anything that looks familiar.

Blazes are marks you leave on trees to mark your way as you hike. Blazes can be made from different things, but bushcrafters like to use charcoal from campfires to mark their way. Simply use a piece of charcoal to mark the fronts and backs of trees as you hike. You can then follow your blazes back to camp!

4. Now take another route in a different direction and do the same thing: mark trees with blazes as you go, and then come back to "home." As you continue going out and coming back to home, you will begin to form a pattern that resembles a sun with rays.

5. Continue traveling in different directions, each time marking the trail with blazes, until you find something that looks familiar like the trail you wandered off of or the road you were dropped off on.

6. If you still can't find anything familiar, follow the blazes to the end of an existing route and continue on the route to extend it, adding more blazes to the trees you pass. Continue expanding your routes until you find something that looks familiar.

7. If you still can't find anything that looks familiar, even after extending your routes, don't panic! Go back to "home" and wait for an adult to find you. Adults can find your "home" because they will be able to follow the blazes you've created.

SETTING UP CAMP

Setting up a bushcraft camp is like creating a home away from home; you just need to decide how you want to do it. In this chapter, you'll learn how to set up several different types of tarp shelters that will protect you from any kind of weather. And if you want to take comfort to the next level, you'll learn how to create a suprisingly comfy debris bed. Or maybe it's a clear night, and you just want to sleep right next to the campfire and under the stars. However you choose to do it, you'll learn how to sleep comfortably, stay warm, and set up your bushcraft home.

CHOOSING AN AWESOME CAMPSITE

Finding your own campsite in the woods is fun and exciting. Often, if you find a favorite spot, you can return to it over and over again. Just picking any random spot isn't a good idea, though. There are a few things to think about that will make your campsite even more awesome and also ensure it's safe.

WATCH OUT FOR THE FIVE W'S: WIND, WATER, WIDOW-MAKERS, WOOD, AND WILDLIFE

There are five important factors to keep in mind when picking a location for your campsite: wind, water, widow-makers, wood, and wildlife. Keeping these factors in mind will help you pick a safe spot where you can set up camp.

Wind Staying out of the wind is important; wind can make you cold or make campfire embers blow all over. Wind can also blow campfire smoke in your face. Look for a location that is out of the wind. A site that has trees, bushy areas, or other natural windbreaks will help reduce the amount of wind that will be hitting you and your campsite.

Water Make sure you aren't setting up camp in a location where water is going to collect. (Sleeping in a puddle is never fun!) Look for locations that are on high ground and not low spots in a forest, which can be natural collection areas for rainwater. Also, make sure there is a source of water, such as a stream or lake, near your camp so you'll have lots of drinking water and maybe even a fun place to swim!

Widow-makers This is a term the old-timers used. A widow is someone who was once married, but whose partner died. Widow-makers in the woods are trees or dead branches that could fall over, or break, and seriously injure you. Before setting up camp, scan the perimeter of the camp and check the trees above the site to ensure there aren't any dead trees or branches that could fall or break off in a wind storm. If you see any of these near your site, find another spot.

Wood Having firewood is important. How are you going to stay warm or cook without a campfire?! Look for a location that has plenty of dead branches and sticks on the ground that can be chopped up and used for your campfires.

Wildlife Make sure you know what types of animals are in the area. Bears, skunks, and deer can all be common in many areas of North America, so you'll want to know what to expect before you ever leave for your trip. Depending on where you are camping, you may need to secure your food in a tree or a special barrel (called a *bear barrel)* so animals don't come into your camp and eat your marshmallows or other snacks.

RESPECTING MOTHER NATURE (LEAVING NO TRACE)

When you go into the woods, remember that you are a visitor. The wilderness is home to countless plants, animals, and insects, and it's important to leave their home just the way you found it when you arrived. Leaving no trace means that when you leave camp, it looks just the same as it did when you first arrived.

- *Always respect wildlife.* You are hanging out in their home, so don't destroy their property. Bird nests are cool, but they are also where birds live, so don't rip them out of trees. Also, don't kill insects if they are just passing through or if you just happen to see one.

- *Minimize campfires.* Campfires are one of the best parts of being outdoors, but you don't need to make huge campfires. Large campfires are often just a waste of fuel and can also leave destruction behind. Small, reasonably sized campfires are best. And if you use rocks to make a campfire ring, return the rocks to where you found them when you're done at the site.

- *Never leave behind any garbage.* If you can carry it in, you can carry it out. Remember that other people want to enjoy the outdoors too, and looking at trash on the ground isn't enjoyable for anyone. You can also help keep natural spaces clean by carrying a few extra trash bags with you to camp. After you've cleaned up your own site, pick up any trash you find as you exit the woods.

- *Never dump chemicals of any type in water or on the ground.* Chemicals like tool oil and bug spray can contaminate areas where insects and wildlife live, and they can also contaminate water sources.

BE WISE WHEN CUTTING LIVE TREES AND BRANCHES

At times, bushcraft projects will require you to use plants and trees, and some projects will require "green wood," which is living plant material. Some projects might also require several small branches, and while it might be tempting to cut live trees for every project, particularly if it's proving difficult to find lots of dead material, doing so isn't always good for the environment. Many of the skills bushcrafters practice today for fun and comfort are the same skills that were used during the 1700s and 1800s when men, women, and children lived in the woods and had to do some of these same things just to survive. Because we do this today as a hobby, it's important that we make as little impact on the environment as possible when we're out in the woods. If you do have to cut any live branches or trees, try to make good decisions on what should be cut. Using small trees that are located under large, healthy trees is a good start. Many of these small trees are likely to die because the larger trees take up most of the sunlight and ground nutrients the smaller trees would need to survive, so they're perfect for bushcraft projects. Leave larger trees and smaller trees in open areas be, and try to use as much dead and fallen wood in your projects as possible.

PROJECT: LEAN-TO TARP SHELTER

The lean-to tarp shelter is used in cold weather. The back blocks the wind, and the campfire heat from the front is trapped in the shelter and warms it up. While it may seem like you might get wet in a shelter like this, that usually isn't the case; this setup can keep you pretty dry and comfortable.

If you use a heavier tarp, you may need to secure the middle of the tarp on the ridgeline with an additional line. To do this, use another trucker's hitch to tie the center of the tarp off to a tree directly behind the shelter.

SETUP

1 Set up a ridgeline, which is a rope that is strung between two trees. Use a trucker's hitch knot to make the ridgeline tight around each tree.

2 Use two smaller pieces of rope to create two prusik loop knots on the ridgeline. Once the knots are in place, use clove hitch knots to affix two small sticks (also referred to as *toggles*) to the ends of each prusik line.

3 Attach two corners of the tarp to the ridgeline using the toggles. Slide the prusik knots away from each other to make the tarp tight.

4 Use tent pegs to secure the bottom corners of the tarp to the ground.

PROJECT: PLOWPOINT TARP SHELTER

A plowpoint shelter is particularly effective in bad weather and simple to set up. It can block a lot of wind and also block rain that is changing directions. The plowpoint will also trap some heat from a fire, but not quite as much heat as the lean-to shelter.

SETUP

1 Using a piece of rope and a square knot, tie one corner of the tarp to a tree at about chest height.

2 Stake out the three remaining corners of the tarp to the ground with tent pegs. (It's that simple!)

PROJECT:
A-FRAME TARP
SHELTER

The A-frame shelter has been used by camping enthusiasts for decades. It's designed to be used without fire and is intended to provide extreme protection from rain, wind, and snow. Be sure to position it correctly to block the wind. If you don't, the wind will blow through your shelter all night, and you won't sleep well.

1 Set up a ridgeline between two trees. Use a trucker's hitch to attach the ridgeline to the trees.

2 Drape the tarp across the ridgeline so equal amounts of the tarp are hanging on each side. If the tarp has loops for securing it to the ridgeline, tie two prusik knots to the ridgeline, and affix toggles to the ends of the prusik knots. Slide the toggles through the loops and then slide the prusik knots away from each other to tighten the tarp.

3 Stake out the four corners of the tarp with tent pegs.

PROJECT: WILDERNESS MATTRESS

Sleeping on the ground can be uncomfortable! And in cold weather, sleeping on bare ground can make you even colder, so making a wilderness mattress to sleep on is well worth the effort. A wilderness mattress, or *debris bed,* uses only found materials and is perfect for making a comfortable foundation to sleep on.

SETUP

1 Place large logs on each side of the mattress area; these logs should be longer than your body. Place smaller logs across the ends of the larger logs to create a rectangular frame. (The frame will help keep the debris inside the frame. You can build a mattress without a frame, but the debris will move throughout the night and you'll likely wake up on the dirt with the debris around you.)

2 Fill the frame with debris like dry leaves, pine needles, and pine tree branches. (It's important to make the mattress foundation very thick. When you lay on it and the debris is compressed, there should still be about 6 to 8 inches (15cm to 20cm) of material between you and the ground.) Top the foundation with softer materials like dry leaves and grasses.

TIPS FOR SLEEPING IN THE OUTDOORS

Sleeping in the outdoors may feel a little uncomfortable at first, but you'll find out very quickly that it can be one of the most relaxing nights of sleep you'll ever have—and it's fun! Sleeping under the stars and listening to the night music of the forest is an unforgettable experience. Here are some basic tips to ensure you'll stay dry, be comfortable, and sleep well.

IF IT'S COLD...

- Wear a loose-fitting beanie. A hat will prevent you from losing a lot of heat and will keep you warmer.

- If it's really cold, you should use a sleeping bag that is rated for the temperatures you'll be sleeping in. If it's not too cold, you can use a wool blanket as a sleeping bag.

- Go to the bathroom before you go to sleep. If you have to urinate at night, your body has to keep the urine warm. If you don't have a lot of urine in you when you go to sleep, that heat can be used by your body elsewhere.

- Wear *loose* socks. Tight socks can cut off the circulation in your feet, making your toes cold.

- Put a bottle of warm water inside an extra sock and put it inside your blanket. It will act like a heater.

IF IT'S WARM...

- In very warm weather, position your shelter so you catch some, but not all, of the wind. A light breeze will keep you cool.

- Hang a bug net or a piece of very fine netting over the open ends of your shelter to help prevent mosquito bites.

- Consider using a cotton bed sheet or fleece blanket instead of a wool blanket. They will still keep you warm, but not so warm that you will be sweating.

- A hammock strung between two trees will keep you away from crawling insects, and the breeze blowing under the hammock will keep you cool all night long.

- Before going to sleep, wipe your face, neck, and arms with a towel dipped in cold water. This will make you feel cool and refreshed.

USING WOOL BLANKETS

Now that you have a roof over your head and a mattress to sleep on, you need a cover. Behold! The wool blanket! Wool blankets are very traditional camping covers and a favorite of bushcrafters. Wool keeps its insulative value even when it's wet, and since wool fibers are hollow, they trap heat while wicking moisture away from your body. Here are a few secrets to using a wool blanket to keep you extra warm and comfortable.

WEAR IT LIKE A COAT

You can wear a wool blanket like a coat to keep you extra warm, even when you're sleeping. Wrap it around your shoulders or over your head, and you'll be amazed at how warm it will keep you. If you have a blanket pin (pictured) or even a large safety pin, you can secure the blanket so you don't have to hold it closed the entire time.

FUN FACT!

Even when wet, wool stays warm. It's a natural fiber that holds in heat and blocks outside weather. It's also flame retardant, so it won't get damaged if small embers from a campfire happen to crackle onto your blanket.

MAKE A
SLEEPING BAG

If it's not too cold, you can turn your wool blanket into a sleeping bag. All you need is a large wool blanket, a large straight needle, and some polyester thread. Fold the blanket in half and sew a running stitch along the bottom and side of the blanket to enclose it. (See chapter 9 to learn how to make the stitch.) You can then easily remove the stitch.

PROJECT: WOOL BLANKET BURRITO

Simply throwing a wool blanket over top of you means a lot of extra material will be lying on the ground, which isn't going to help keep you warm. By wrapping yourself up in your blanket like a burrito, you get the most warmth potential out of your wool blanket. The first few times you try this, you might need some help, but you'll eventually master it and be able to do it yourself.

1 Lay the blanket on the ground like a diamond, and then lie on the blanket with your head at the top of the diamond and your feet at the bottom. (This will add a layer of warmth underneath you.)

2 Pull the bottom of the diamond up over your knees.

3 Take one corner of the blanket and pull it across your body, and then tuck it underneath your body. This will add a layer of wool on top of you and another layer underneath you.

4 Pull the opposite corner of the blanket across, and tuck it under your body. You will then have two layers of wool on top of you and three underneath you.

5 Roll up the point above your head to create a headrest. (If it gets really cold, you can pull the top part of the blanket over your head.)

STARTING A CAMPFIRE

A campfire is absolutely essential and is the heart of the camp: it's where everyone cooks their food, warms up, and hangs out in the evenings. Firemaking is one of the most enjoyable tasks you'll perform at camp, and there are dozens of ways to start a campfire, but in this chapter you'll learn some of the best ways to get a fire going and also keep it going. Once you've built a few of your own fires, you'll be able to decide your favorite way of building one.

THE TRIANGLE OF FIRE

The process of building a campfire is similar to the process of cooking—if you add the right ingredients and follow the steps, you'll end up with a successful meal. In much the same way, if have the right ingredients for a fire and follow the steps, you'll build a successful campfire every time. If a fire won't start, it's likely because you're missing a key ingredient.

THE KEY INGREDIENTS FOR FIRE

A campfire is made up of three key ingredients: heat, fuel, and oxygen, which together are known as the *triangle of fire*. What's cool is that no matter where you live or what the weather may be like, these three ingredients will never change, and they can always be used to start a good campfire.

Heat

Heat can come from a variety of sources, including matches, a ferro rod, a spark from a steel striker, or even the sun.

Fuel

Fuel is what's going to burn in the campfire. Typically, this is dry wood that you'll gather. Wood comes in all different shapes and sizes, but it's important to match the size of the wood with the size of the fire you're building.

Oxygen

Oxygen is important for your fire to survive and thrive, and a good fire needs the perfect amount of oxygen. If there isn't enough oxygen because you've piled too many sticks on top of the fire, it will be smothered and will extinguish. If the fire starts, but the the flame isn't protected and the wind is blowing too hard, the flame will blow out. If you create an environment where the flame is protected and still has access to sufficient oxygen, you're going to have a successful fire.

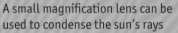

COOL TIP!

A small magnification lens can be used to condense the sun's rays into a bright, hot beam that can ignite dry tinder like grasses to start a fire.

COLLECTING FIREWOOD

Collecting wood for a campfire is one of the most important and time-consuming parts of fire building, so it's something you'll need to practice. Beginners often will pick up any wood they find on the forest floor and try to make it work, but that wood may be too wet to burn. Choosing the right type of wood for your campfire will make all the difference in how easily your fire starts, and also how well it burns.

HOW TO FIND GOOD FIREWOOD

The most important thing to remember when looking for firewood is that dry wood will burn, while wet wood will smolder and flicker out. Any wet wood you gather will need to be dried out before it can burn, which means that the small flame you will be using to try to start your campfire will also need to dry out all the moisture in the wood before it can burn, and this is pretty difficult to do. Gathering dry wood eliminates this problem and allows the flame to grow faster and burn hotter. Here are some simple tips that will help you find good, burnable wood for your campfire.

Do...

- **...look for dead branches that are sitting off the ground.** Quite often, branches that break off a tree will be caught in other branches or in low vegetation. These pieces will be drier than anything you will find on the ground and will provide perfect fuel for your fire.

- **...look for dead trees.** Dead trees won't have leaves or needles, and will be shedding bark. If you find a dead tree, grasp a branch and try to break it off. If it breaks off cleanly, you've found good wood. When you break branches from a dead tree, start near the trunk. If the branch snaps away freely, all the outward branches will also be dry. This can save a lot of time!

- **...use the cheek test.** If you're unsure if a branch is too green to burn, place the broken end of the branch against your cheek. If it feels cold, most likely it's too green to burn. The moisture in the wood will create a cooler sensation on your cheek compared to wood that is dry.

- **...gather _lots_ of small sticks.** Always gather extremely small sticks to get the fire going, and gather as many as you can find. Small sticks are easier to light than large logs. And even small sticks that are slightly wet can dry out quickly from a small flame and still light. As a fire grows, larger sticks can be added to build the fire.

- **...match wood size to flame size.** A good thing to remember is that small sticks like small flames and large sticks like large flames. If your heat source is small, you should start your fire using only small sticks. Once the fire grows larger, you can add larger pieces of wood.

Don't...

- **...use wood from the ground.** The ground contains moisture that is absorbed by the wood, which will leave it wet.

- **...pick green wood.** Green wood is wood that comes from live trees. Trees with leaves or needles on them are still growing, and live trees are full of water and moisture.

- **...gather sticks that bend but don't break.** Test the sticks you pick up by trying to break them. If they snap easily, they're dry enough to burn. If they only bend or just crack, the wood is likely still green and not good for campfires.

MAKING HOMEMADE FIRE EXTENDERS

Along with a heat source such as a ferro rod or matches, it's important to have something that will burn longer in order to get the fire going and get your wood burning. These long-burning items are called *fire extenders* and they extend how long the first flame burns. There are many natural fire extenders in the woods, but it's always a good idea to be prepared and carry some along with you as you head into the woods. Making fire extenders at home can be super fun and will get your campfires burning faster.

LAUNDRY DRYER LINT

Do you sometimes complain that you have to do laundry? Well, maybe you should rethink that! There is something called a *lint trap* in a clothes dryer, and this trap collects the lint from clothes as they dry. This lint just happens to also be a great fire extender; it lights and burns easily. You can collect it in a resealable bag and take it along to your campsite. When you're ready to start a campfire, simply ball it up and ignite it.

Laundry dryer lint

COTTON BALL GOOP

To make cotton ball goop, you'll need some cotton balls and petroleum jelly (Vaseline). Dip the cotton balls in the petroleum jelly and store them in a jar or an old pill bottle. These balls will light easily and burn for a long time.

Cotton ball goop

DUCT TAPE

Duct tape is made of a woven fabric that has a sticky adhesive applied to it. To use it as a fire extender, shred the tape into small strips to expose the fibers. The fibers and the sticky adhesive are both flammable, which means they will burn. (Duct tape is also good for fixing your gear.)

Duct tape

FLAMING DISKS

These fire extenders require some effort to make, but they are the best option. You will need flat cotton disks, wax, and lighter fluid. Working outdoors and with adult supervision, melt some wax in a dish and then add an equal amount of lighter fluid. Dip the cotton disks into the mixture, allow the excess to run off, and then set the disks on aluminum foil to dry. These disks are waterproof, will burn for over three minutes, and are easy to pack. To use, partially tear the disk to expose the cotton fibers, and then ignite the disk with your heat source.

Flaming disks

NATURAL FIRE EXTENDERS

Mother nature always provides everything we need, and that includes fire extenders! These natural fire extenders will work just as well as any options we can buy or make at home, so if you can find these around your campsite, they'll work great for getting your fire going. Note that you should still pack homemade fire extenders because not all locations will have these materials.

BIRCH BARK

The bark from birch trees provides a great way to make a fire. The bark contains an oil that repels water to keep the thin bark dry and burnable. The oil is also flammable, so it's perfect to use as a fire extender. Simply pull the bark off the tree in strips and ignite it. It will burn long, and it works well in wet weather.

Birch bark

DRIED GRASSES

Dried grasses can work as fire extenders, but they aren't always the best options. In dry environments, dried grasses can light quickly and easily. Some grasses, though, have tube-like sections that can hold moisture. If you can't find other options, give this one a try.

Dried grasses

FATWOOD

Pine trees are full of sticky sap, and wood saturated with this sap is an excellent fire extender. The sap flows throughout the tree, and when the tree dies, the sap starts to flow back down to the ground. But because it's so sticky, it sometimes can cause a clog in the tree (much like a clogged pipe in a house), and that sap has nowhere to go and accumulates where branches meet the trunk of the tree. This burnable material is called *fatwood,* and the wood will look gold and orange, and also smell odd. To use fatwood, cut or break the branch from the tree, and when you're ready to light your fire, shave the fatwood into a pile.

TREE BARK

While many trees do not have bark that can be used as a fire extender, some trees, such as poplar, basswood, and cedar, have bark that will work great for starting fires. It's not difficult to figure out which trees have usable fuel. Some tree bark is crunchy and breaks into small pieces, and that is *not* what you want to use. Other trees, however, have bark that has fibers that look like they're made of threads or small pieces of rope. These pieces won't break apart, but rather will pull away into thin strips, and this is what you're looking for. Just squish the strips into a ball, and it will light quickly and easily.

Fatwood

Tree bark

WOOD SHAVINGS

Sometimes everything in the woods is wet because it has been raining or snowing. How can you find anything dry to burn in these conditions? Simple! Find a dead stick and use your knife to peel way the bark. While the bark will be wet, the inside will likely still be dry and can be cut into small shavings, like toothpicks or even finer shavings. These dry pieces of wood will burn with ease!

SETTING UP
A FIRE LAY

Once you have a way to make heat and you've collected your firewood, it's time to build the fire lay. The fire lay describes whatever method you use to organize the sticks to ensure they burn efficiently. While building a campfire might seem as simple as just throwing sticks on a flame, making a good fire lay is key to creating a fire that will burn for a long period of time.

TEEPEE METHOD

The teepee method isn't the most efficient way to start a fire. If you don't have good wood or your flame goes out, you may need to reconfigure the structure, which can be difficult if some of the wood is still hot. This method is best used once you have a strong fire burning and you want to add larger sticks. The structure will then create large, high flames.

LOG CABIN METHOD

To make a log cabin fire, simply stack the sticks as if you are building a cabin, and then light a fire inside the "walls." The walls can collapse with this method and it doesn't always light easily, so if you try this, make sure to continuously add small sticks while the initial flame burns. Once you have a large fire inside the cabin, the outside walls should catch fire.

TIPS FOR KEEPING YOUR CAMPFIRE BURNING

- If the flame begins to die after you've added more sticks, simply remove the new sticks, and the fire should return to its previous state. Slowly begin adding the sticks back to the fire.
- Be patient during wet weather. The sticks you place on the fire might take longer to ignite, and that's okay. Just be patient, and wait until they're burning before adding the next layer of sticks.
- If you add the first pile of sticks and the flame begins to die down and looks like it might go out, simply lift the backstop upward. (The backstop is explained in the following pages.) This will increase the amount of oxygen to the flame and help it burn stronger.

STACK METHOD

There are many different styles of fire lays, but the stack method is the best. Other methods require that the entire fire lay is built before the fire is started, but the stack method allows you to make adjustments as you move along and gives you greater control over the fire as you build it.

1 Gather sticks of varying sizes, and sort them into piles by size. (Remember to look for dry sticks that snap easily.)

2 Build a backstop using a large stick or a pile of sticks placed toward the back of the fire-building area. This backstop will keep oxygen flowing to the flame and also prevent the sticks from smothering the flame. Build a platform next to the backstop that will keep the wood you're burning elevated and dry. (A platform is simply a stick or group of sticks that are placed on the wet ground to create a dry area for your first flame.) If the sticks you're using for your platform are really wet, use an axe to split a stick into two halves to reveal the dry inside surface. You can then use this dry surface area to ignite your flame. Place your fire extender on top of the dry platform.

3 Light the fire extender and let it begin to burn. The fire extender should be placed close to the backstop and on top of the platform. (Note that you should never blow on an open flame; only blow on an ember when making a fire. If you have a flame, you've already completed the triangle of fire and just need to add fuel. Adding oxygen will only blow out the flame!)

4 Once the fire extender is burning, begin adding small sticks over the fire extender, making sure to rest the sticks on the backstop to prevent the sticks from smothering the fire extender. (It's important not to add too many sticks at once, but also not to add too few. An amount equal to what you can hold in your hand is about right.)

5 Once the first pile of small sticks begins to burn, slowly add more small sticks directly on top of the burning sticks.

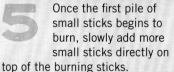

6 Continue adding sticks. Remember that the larger the flame, the larger the sticks you should add.

STARTING A CAMPFIRE WITH MATCHES

Matches provide an instant flame, but they can extinguish quickly, so starting a campfire with them can be challenging unless you know how to do it correctly. Making something called a *stick bundle* will help you get a campfire started with just one match. A stick bundle is like a handheld fire lay, and it's a very effective way to start a campfire.

COOL TIP!

Look for evergreen trees when searching for small sticks for burning. They have the smallest, thinnest branches of any tree, and they're perfect for starting campfires.

HOW TO START A MATCH FIRE WITH A STICK BUNDLE

Making a stick bundle and lighting it with a single match is super easy. Here's how you do it.

1 Collect enough extremely small-diameter sticks that you can hold them all in one hand. (Sticks the diameter of toothpicks are ideal.) Arrange the sticks so that the small ends are all pointing in the same direction and the larger ends are pointing in the opposite direction. Snap the sticks in half and place the small ends with the other small ends. This will be your stick bundle.

2 Hold the bundle upright in your hand with the small ends of the bundle pointing downward. Ignite your match and place it directly beneath the bundle. As the match burns, slowly push it up into the stick bundle until the sticks begin to burn. Once the bundle is burning, carefully place the burning side of the bundle down into your fire lay with the larger ends resting on the backstop of the fire lay. Now you can begin building your fire using the stack method.

STARTING A CAMPFIRE WITH A FERRO ROD

A ferrocerium rod, also known as a *ferro rod,* is the ultimate survival fire starter. It can start fires in both cold and wet weather conditions and will work for a very long time. Scraping a ferro rod with a sharp object creates extremely hot sparks that will ignite homemade fire extenders as well as natural materials like fatwood, birch bark, and dried grass.

COOL TIP!

If you lose the striker that comes with the ferro rod, you can use the back of the saw that comes with a multi-tool as a striker. It's usually sharp enough to create good sparks from the rod.

HOW TO START A FIRE USING A FERRO ROD

Starting a fire with a ferro rod requires a rod as well as a good striker, which is any tool or object that is sharp enough to scrape material from the rod and make sparks. (Note that you should *never* use your knife edge to do this; the rod will damage your knife blade.) Here's how to start a fire using a ferro rod.

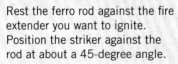 Rest the ferro rod against the fire extender you want to ignite. Position the striker against the rod at about a 45-degree angle.

2 Using heavy force, scrape downward on the rod with the striker until you see sparks. Continue scraping with force until the extender is ignited. (Don't worry if it takes a few strikes to generate sparks and ignite the extender; this is common.)

TIPS FOR USING A FERRO ROD

- Removing material from the ferro rod is what causes the sparks, so try to remove as much material as possible with each strike.
- Pressure is more important than speed. Don't be concerned with how fast you can strike the rod, instead focus on how hard you can push the striker against the rod.
- If you can't get good sparks by pushing the striker down the rod, try pulling the rod back while pushing the striker forward.

STARTING A CAMPFIRE WITH FLINT AND STEEL

The flint-and-steel fire starting method is a traditional way of making fire that was once used by long hunters and mountain men. It's the bushcraft go-to way to make a fire, but more importantly, it's an extremely fun way to create a fire! (Note that it's really important that you have an adult help you with this, so don't try it unless there is an adult present to supervise.)

HOW TO USE FLINT AND STEEL TO START A CAMPFIRE

For this method, you'll need a steel striker, a very sharp hard rock (typically referred to as a *flint*), and char cloth, which is a special cloth you'll create. You'll also need some shredded inner tree bark or dried grass to make what is called a *bird's nest*, which is what will be ignited by the burning char cloth. (Char cloth is a burnt material that will ignite when a spark hits it. You will learn how to create your own char cloth in the pages that follow.)

1 Collect some good fire starting material like dried grass or shredded inner tree bark. Squish the material into a ball that is at least the size of a baseball. Make the ball dense enough that you can't see through it.

2 Using your thumb, form a small divot in the ball to create a "bird's nest."

3 Hold the steel striker in your dominant hand (the one you write with), and hold the flint in the opposite hand. With your dominant hand, flick your wrist so the striker comes in contact with the stone. (It's important to not smash the steel into the stone but rather skim the striker off the stone. Imagine you are cutting little pieces of metal off the striker with the stone.) If you aren't getting sparks, try holding the stone at a 45-degree angle or adjust the stone so a sharper edge is pointing at the striker. This will make the sparks fly!

Once you get good sparks, add a folded piece of char cloth on top of the stone. Position the char cloth right against the edge of the stone, and then strike the stone with your striker. The goal is to have a spark land on the char cloth and ignite it. When sparks do land on the char cloth, immediately add oxygen by blowing into the char cloth.

4 Once the char cloth is ignited, immediately place the burning ember in the divot in the "bird's nest."

5 Begin blowing into the "bird's nest." You will notice the material begin to smoke and glow.

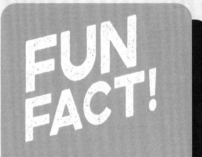

6 Once the fire extender is burning, place the "bird's nest" into your fire lay and begin adding sticks. Now you've made your first flint and steel fire! Super exciting, right?!

FUN FACT!

The stone is cutting metal away from your steel striker, so the striker is what is sparking, not the stone!

HOW TO MAKE CHAR CLOTH

Making char cloth is super easy. All you'll need is a tin or steel container with a tight-fitting lid and some 100-percent cotton material. (Terry cloth is the ideal choice.) Place the material in the container and seal it tightly so no air can get in. Now just throw it into the campfire! That's right! Just throw the container right into the campfire. After 10 to 15 minutes, use some sticks to carefully remove the container from the fire, being very careful not to burn yourself.

Allow the container to cool completely before opening it. (If you open the tin while it's still hot, oxygen will be added to the recipe and the char cloth could ignite, so be sure to keep the tin closed until it is completely cooled.) Once the tin has cooled, remove the lid. The cotton material should be completely black but not burned up. If it's just brown, replace the lid and throw the container back into the campfire and cook it for another 10 to 15 minutes or until the cloth is completely black. You can't overcook char!

While small sparks won't always light fire extenders, small sparks will ignite char cloth, so it's good to make this at camp!

FUN FACT!

Remember the triangle of fire? Heat, oxygen, and fuel are the three things required to make fire. Now think about what happens when you make char cloth. You had heat from the campfire and fuel from the cotton material, but there wasn't any oxygen because the fuel was inside the container and oxygen couldn't get to it. Because of this, the cotton will "cook" in the campfire and become carbon, but it won't actually burn because there isn't any oxygen in the container.

7

MAKING CAMP COMFORTABLE

You've got your sleeping area set up and have a fire going; now it's time to make camp even more like home. In this chapter, you'll learn how to make all kinds of useful things, including unique cooking configurations as well as useful items like hooks to hold your gear and a boot dryer to keep your boots dry. You'll also learn how to make a workbench along with supplies like rope, tent pegs, and clothespins, that you may have forgotten when you left home. Building items to make camp more comfortable is one of the most fun and creative parts of being a bushcrafter.

PROJECT: BRANCH HOOK

Don't let your gear lie in the mud or dirt. Hang it up! This super cool branch hook is easy and fun to make. You can make multiple hooks and hang them all around your camp.

1 Using a folding saw, cut a "Y" branch that is about 1 inch (2.5cm) in diameter, approximately 8 inches (20.5cm) long, and straight on one side. Be sure to cut a green branch and not a dead branch; a dead branch will not be strong enough to hold the weight of your gear.

 Using your knife, very carefully split the branch down the straight side so it's flat on that side.

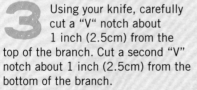 Using your knife, carefully cut a "V" notch about 1 inch (2.5cm) from the top of the branch. Cut a second "V" notch about 1 inch (2.5cm) from the bottom of the branch.

Using twine, tightly secure the branch to a tree. Make sure the twine is secured in the two "V" notches to ensure the hook doesn't slip.

PROJECT: TENT PEGS

Bushcrafters don't always carry tent pegs. Why? Because we like to make them! There are two unique ways to make tent pegs and both are fun bushcraft projects.

STRAIGHT PEG

1 Using a camp saw, cut a straight green stick that's about the thickness of your index finger and about 8 inches (20.5cm) long.

2 Using your camp knife, carve one end of the stick to a sharp point and then round off the other end.

3 Cut a "seven" notch 1 inch (2.5cm) from the rounded end. (A "seven" notch is flat on one end and angled on the other.) Make sure the flat end of the notch is closest to the rounded end of the peg.

FUN FACT!

If you round the end of a tent peg, it's less likely to split when you hammer it into the ground.

"Y" PEG

1 Choose a "Y" branch that is about the thickness of your index finger and about 8 inches (20.5cm) long. Be sure to cut a green branch and not a dead branch: a dead branch will break when you pound the peg into the ground.

2 Using a folding saw, cut the branch about 1 inch (2.5cm) below the "V."

3 Cut the "Y" ray that extends away from the branch to a length of about 1 inch (2.5cm).

4 Using your knife, sharpen the longest "Y" ray so the point easily goes into the ground, and then use your knife to round off the remaining ends.

PROJECT: BOOT DRYERS

Wet boots at camp can make a day miserable. And during colder months, it's really important to dry your boots at camp so your feet do not get cold. These super simple boot dryers are an easy way to keep your boots dry. Placing your boots upside down allows gravity to draw the moisture out of your boots.

COOL TIP!

You can make the "Y" branches and straight sticks longer and then start a small fire next to your boots to dry them more quickly. Just be careful to place them far enough away from the fire that they don't melt or catch on fire! (It's best to place the boots next to the fire and not directly over it.)

1 Using a folding saw, cut two "Y" branches that are about 12 inches (30cm) long. Carve a sharp point at the bottom of each branch.

2 Cut two more straight sticks that are about the same length as the "Y" branches. Carve a sharp point at the bottom of each of these sticks.

3 Push the "Y" branches into the ground, and then push the straight sticks into the ground at distances equal to about the length of your boots.

4 Place the backs of the boots (where your feet go into the boots) on the straight sticks, and then place the toes of the boots onto the "Y" branches.

PROJECT:
FIREWOOD
CARRIER

Small wood is the key to a good campfire: small sticks help start the fire and also help get the fire going again once it has burned down to embers. But carrying lots of small sticks can be challenging unless you know this little bushcraft trick.

1 Using a folding saw, cut two straight sticks that are each about the diameter of your thumb and about 2 feet (61cm) in length.

Use the saw to cut "V" notches at the ends of the sticks that are about 3 inches (7.5cm) from each end. (These "V" notches will help the ropes stay in place.)

Lay the two sticks parallel to each other and about 3 feet (91cm) apart. Cut two long pieces of rope that are each 3.5 feet (1m) long, and place the rope pieces underneath the sticks. Use slip knots to tie the sticks together, making sure to secure the rope in the "V" notches.

Place your collected wood across the two pieces of rope and in the middle of the carrier.

When you're ready to haul, pull one of the firewood carrier sticks across the wood stack, tuck it behind the ropes, and carry the wood back to camp!

PROJECT: WORKBENCH

Every job requires tools, as well as a place to use those tools safely and effectively, so having a sturdy work area at camp is important. This handy workbench will give you the perfect workspace for cutting sticks and chopping logs. It's also helpful for holding round sticks as you're cutting them or for making more precise cuts or carvings.

1 Find a large fallen tree that is located slightly away from the camp area. (You will be using axes, knives, and saws in this area, so having it farther away from camp will make it safer for everyone.) Make sure the downed tree isn't rotten and is stable enough that it doesn't move when you press down on it. If it moves, try stabilizing it with some rocks or by cutting away some limbs.

2 Using your axe, carefully chip away an area on top of the tree trunk to create a flat workspace. This will give you a flat work area to place items on so they won't roll when you're working with them.

3 Using a bow saw or folding saw, cut a large "V" notch into the log. This "V" notch will be useful for holding round sticks and preventing them from rolling as you're cutting them.

4 Using a bow saw or folding saw, cut two notches about 6 inches (15cm) apart and about 2 to 4 inches (5 to 10cm) deep. Use your axe to shave away the area between the notches. This will create another flat work area.

5 Once you have created the square notch, cut some wooden wedges that can be used to hold a workpiece securely against the sides of the square notch.

PROJECT:
BARK BASKET

Barks baskets are fun to make and can be made in several different sizes. They're very handy for collecting nuts and berries, or even for carrying your gear. Note that not every tree bark can be used for this project. Barks from tulip, poplar, and birch trees are fibrous, flexible, and will work well.

1 Using a knife or folding saw, cut a rectangular area in the bark of the tree that is the width you desire the basket to be and then cut it to be about twice the height of the basket you want to finish with. (You will be folding the bark in half.) Once you've cut through the bark, use your fingers or a stick to pry the bark from the tree.

2 Place the bark piece on a flat work surface. Find the center point on each of the long sides, and then mark those points. Starting at one center point, use your knife to mark out a football shape from one center point to the center point on the opposite side, being careful to only cut the outer bark. (If you cut all the way through, you will ruin the basket.)

3 Carefully fold the two ends of the bark together. (The football shape you cut into the bark will serve as the bottom of the basket.)

4 Wrap a long, thin, fibrous strip of bark or a piece of thin rope around the top of the basket to create a top ring that will hold the basket together.

COOL TIP!

If you're making a larger basket, you can cut holes up both sides of the basket and lace them closed. It will make the basket look much nicer and also hold it together better.

PROJECT: HOT WOOD TONGS

Moving burning wood around a campfire is a chore and can also be dangerous—hot wood can burn you and result in a fun trip ending very quickly. Fortunately, there's a very easy way to move hot sticks and logs around a campfire, and it requires just a few simple steps. These tongs work like cooking tongs, only for wood!

1 Cut a straight stick that is about 1 inch (2.5cm) in diameter and about 3 feet (1m) long. Cut a second stick that is a "Y" branch, about 1 inch (2.5cm) in diameter, and about 3 feet (1m) in length.

2 Place the "Y" branch against the firewood piece you want to move, and then insert the straight stick through the "Y" branch and over the piece of firewood. Grasp the top ends of both sticks and pull them together to pinch the hot firewood. This will allow you to move the firewood with ease.

PROJECT: ROOT ROPE

What happens if you get to camp and realize you don't have any rope? Don't worry! If you're in a pinch, roots from several different types of trees and plants will work really well as rope.

If you're not going to use the roots right away, try to keep them wet until you're ready to use them. Once the roots dry, they will shrink and become very tight around whatever you've tied them around.

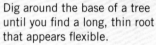 Dig around the base of a tree until you find a long, thin root that appears flexible.

2 Dig along the root until you come to the end. If you can easily break the root free, it might be too small and fragile, but if you need to cut it free, you've probably picked a good root to use.

3 Split a small green stick into two halves and then place the root between the two flat sides of the split sticks. Squeeze the sticks together, and then pull the root through to remove the outer coating. (You can also remove the outer coating by picking it off with your fingers, but using the sticks makes it easier.)

4 Once you've removed the outer coating, you've got a replacement for thin, lightweight rope that will work very well.

PROJECT: NATURAL TWINE

Remember when we talked about finding fibrous inner tree bark to make a bird's nest for starting a fire? You can use that very same material to make natural twine. Just like root rope, natural twine can be used for a variety of projects and can also be used to make heavier rope for more heavy-duty projects.

1 Gather several long strands of inner tree bark. You'll want to gather a lot of bark, depending on how much twine you want to make. Note that you should keep the strands damp while making the twine or they will shrink and stiffen.

2 Holding one strand of bark with both hands, twist the right end continuously until the strand kinks and twists over on itself to a form a loop.

3 Grasp the twisted loop with your left hand and then pinch the right end of the strand between your thumb and index finger. Twist the right strand inward and to the left until it's tight.

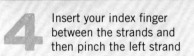

4 Insert your index finger between the strands and then pinch the left strand between your index finger and thumb.

5 Turn your hand to twist both ends together. Repeat the process, twisting the right end inward and then turning your hand to twist both ends together.

6 When you get close to completing a strand, fold another strand in half, place it between the two open ends, and twist it into the line. To finish the line, tie off the ends with straight lashings.

PROJECT: ROPE SPINNER

Sometimes you need to make heavier rope for bigger projects. You may need to tie up a shelter or set up a heavy tripod to hang gear on. If don't have good, strong rope for the job, you'll be out of luck. Using natural twine and this handy rope spinner, you'll be able to spin a heavy-duty rope that is very strong and can handle almost any task that regular rope can handle.

1 Cut two straight sticks, one about 15 inches (38cm) long and about 1.5 inches (4cm) in diameter, and another that is about 6 inches long and about 1 inch (2.5cm) in diameter. Use your axe to split the longer stick down the middle and into two halves.

Using your knife, carefully carve two U-shaped notches about 1 inch (2.5cm) from the bottom ends of the split stick. (When you put the two pieces back together, it should appear as if there is a round hole in the stick.)

Carve enough material away from one end of the smaller stick that it will fit inside the larger stick hole, while still leaving about 1 inch (2.5cm) of material at the end of the stick. You want to remove enough material that the smaller stick will spin freely inside the notch.

Place the two halves of the larger stick back together with the smaller stick secured inside the hole. (If the smaller stick doesn't turn freely inside the notch, you'll need to carve away more material until it spins freely.)

Using straight lashings, lash the larger stick together at both ends, with the smaller stick nested inside the notch.

PROJECT: HEAVY-DUTY ROPE

Now that your rope spinner is complete, it's time to make some rope! You'll need *a lot* of twine to make this rope; the amount of twine you start with will only yield about one-fourth of the same amount as rope. (If you're not able to make twine, you can buy jute twine at any hardware or hobby store.)

1 Tie the ends of the twine together with a simple knot to create a single large loop. Loop one end of the rope over your rope spinner, and anchor the other end over a branch or on a stick held by a campmate.

2 Begin spinning the rope spinner in a *clockwise* direction until the entire loop has a tight twist to it.

3 Holding your rope spinner in your right hand, grasp the twisted twine with your left hand and stretch it out to your left side.

4 Walk to where the twine is anchored. Place the twine that is in your left hand over the anchor point to create a second loop. With the loop in your left hand, walk backward until all the slack is out of the line.

5 Place the new loop over the rope spinner and begin spinning again, this time in a *counterclockwise* direction. Once the line is tightly woven, give it a good tug. (This is called "setting," and it helps bind the fibers.) Tie off both ends with straight lashings.

PROJECT: CLOTHESPIN

Hanging wet clothes and socks at night will make the next morning at camp much more comfortable and also less smelly. You can hang a clothesline between two trees and use a few of these clothespins to keep your clothing dry. And because you're a bushcrafter, you can make the clothespins yourself! Add a few thick rubber bands to your gear list for this project.

1 Cut a straight stick that is about 3 inches (7.5cm) long and about the thickness of your thumb. You'll also need a thick rubber band for this project.

2 Using your knife, carefully split the stick into two halves.

3 On the flat sides of each of the split halves, carve small ramps at one end, and then place the halves back together. The two small, carved ramps should form a "V" shape, which will allow the clothespin to be opened when squeezed.

4 Wrap the rubber band around the sticks at a point just below the "V" shape.

5 Your clothespin is now ready to use. Pinch the clothespin at the end with the "V" shape to open it.

PROJECT: CAMP TOILET

Going to the toilet in the woods can be a little uncomfortable. Not to worry, though! Bushcrafters always find a way to make things easier. You can make a toilet at camp by digging a trench, or what is called a *latrine,* where people can go to the toilet at camp. But adding a few extra bushcraft touches will turn an ordinary latrine into a fairly comfy spot to do your business.

1 Locate a spot far from camp where there is a downed tree. Be sure to choose a location that is far enough away that it offers some privacy for campers and is also far from the water source for your camp.

2 Cut two green wood sticks that are 1 inch (2.5cm) in diameter and about 2 feet (61cm) long. Cut a third stick that is about 18 inches (45cm) long.

3 Cut a 3-foot (1m) section of wood that is 3 to 5 inches (7.5 to 13cm) in diameter. Split this larger piece into two pieces.

4 Insert the longer sticks in the ground, spaced approximately 18 inches (46cm) apart and 2 feet (61cm) from the tree. Use square lashings to lash the shorter stick to the longer sticks.

5 Dig a latrine hole that is 12 to 24 inches (30.5cm to 60cm) deep and 12 to 18 inches (30.5cm to 45cm) wide. Leave the dirt from the hole in a pile next to the hole so campers can easily cover their waste when they're done.

6 Lay the two halves of the larger split stick across the downed tree and on the frame made of the three sticks. This will create a seat with a split in the middle, much like a toilet seat.

7 Cut a short "Y" branch, and stick it into the ground next to the toilet seat. Place the toilet paper on the "Y" branch.

8 Position a camp shovel or sturdy stick next to the dirt pile so you can push dirt back into the pit and cover up anything you've left behind. Now you can poop in comfort!

TIPS FOR GOING TO THE TOILET IN THE WOODS

Here are some important things to remember when going to the toilet in the woods:

- Always take toilet paper when you pack your gear. Using leaves and plants to wipe your backside can cause irritation or even worse. Trust me: you don't want to use poison ivy for toilet paper!

- Keep your toilet paper in a resealable plastic bag so it doesn't get damp and ruined.

- If you don't want to carry toilet paper, you can use biodegradable wipes. They're available at many outdoor stores, are safe for the environment, and typically come in a resealable package.

- Locate your toilet as far away from your camp and camp water source as possible.

- Always cover your waste with dirt. Curious animals can get into anything. And other campers do not want to see anything you've left behind.

- Leave a camp shovel or long, sturdy stick next to the toilet so fellow campers can cover their waste after they go to the toilet.

- Wash your hands with biodegradable soap and water after you use the toilet. It's something you do at home, but in the woods, it's easy to forget.

- If you don't have time or a place to make a bushcraft toilet, you can just dig a latrine and squat over it. Just don't forget to cover it up with dirt. (That's like flushing the toilet at home.)

8

COOKING AT CAMP

Mealtime is one of the most important times at camp; it's when you'll make the delicious, nutritious meals that will fuel your body during your adventures. You already know bushcrafting is about making things, and it's no different when it comes to cooking. Bushcrafters can make cooking systems for cooking virtually anything, and they can also make useful cooking tools like spatulas and whisks. In this chapter, you'll learn how to build a perfect cooking fire, how to set up and use several different cooking systems, and how to make a few handy cooking tools.

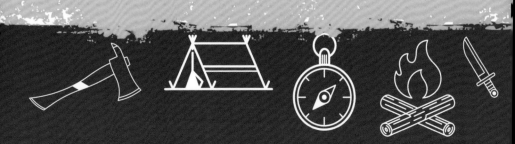

MAKING A CAMPFIRE FOR COOKING

When you think of wood for a campfire, the first thing that might come to mind is piles of neatly stacked wood and a big, roaring fire that will keep you warm. That type of campfire is great for relaxing and staying warm; however, it isn't always the best campfire for cooking. There are different types of fires, and some are better for cooking than others.

FIRE TYPES

Try to think of your cooking campfire like a stove: in order to cook on a stove, you have to be able to control the heat, depending on what you're cooking. If you make macaroni and cheese over high heat, the cheese will burn and the noodles will be undercooked, and the result will not taste very good. You need to use medium to low heat to cook good mac and cheese. The same principle applies to cooking over a campfire. A good cooking fire needs to be controlled, just like on a stove.

Big-flame fire Big-flame fires are best used when the fire is just getting started. The flames are high and very hot, so they're great for boiling liquids, heating up cold meals, melting ice or snow, or building a bed of embers to cook on. To keep big-flame fires going, continuously add a mixture of large and small firewood until the flames are large.

BIG-FLAME FIRE

Medium-flame fire Medium-flame fires are great for simmering stews or soups, preheating cast-iron cookware, or finishing off recipes with an intense burst of heat. Medium-flame fires are actually very easy to maintain. After the initial fire is started, add a generous amount of firewood to make the flames very large, and then just allow the flames to die down as the wood begins to burn up. As the fire dies down, only add one to two pieces of larger split wood at a time. This will keep the flames a few inches high and also keep the heat slightly more consistent.

MEDIUM-FLAME FIRE

Keep adding wood to keep the fire large for about 30 to 60 minutes, and then stop adding wood and let the fire die down. Soon you will be left with only embers.

Hot embers are amazing for cooking all types of meals, and you can cook food directly on them. When doing so, make sure you have a really nice, thick bed of embers. If you see dirt or ash among the embers, you don't have enough. However, if all you see are cherry red embers, the campfire is perfect to cook on. Simply place a piece of meat or a slab of dough directly on the embers. (I recommend using thin pieces of meat or dough in order to cook them thoroughly and quickly.) The heat will cook the food quickly, and the super-hot embers will not stick to the food. Once one side is finished cooking, flip the food over and cook the opposite side.

Small- to no-flame fire A fire usually starts large and extremely hot, but as it dies down, there are pieces of wood that glow red, which are called *embers*. Embers are extremely hot and will remain hot for an extended period of time. The heat they give off is consistent—no hot spots exist—making them perfect for grilling meat, roasting wild game, cooking with a rotisserie, and even cooking directly. To build a small- to no-flame fire, use hardwoods like oak or maple to build a campfire that is extremely large.

SMALL- TO NO-FLAME FIRE

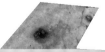

COOKING IN A STEW POT

One traditional way to cook over a campfire is in a stew pot. This method is so easy! For many recipes, you simply toss everything into the pot, place the pot on the embers, and enjoy a delicious meal that doesn't require much cleanup.

HOW TO COOK IN A STEW POT

Cooking in a stew pot is super simple because you don't need anything special to do it—only a small- to medium-flame campfire and a sturdy pot with a lid.

1 Before you stoke the fire, prepare all your ingredients and place them in the pot. Build a small- to medium-flame campfire and allow it to burn down.

2 Once there is a good bed of embers, place the stew pot directly on the embers, but not directly in the fire. As the food begins to cook, move the pot to the side of the campfire so the food still receives heat, but doesn't overboil or burn.

DAN'S WICKED WHITE CHILI

2 tbsp cooking oil (vegetable, canola, etc.)
1 medium onion, chopped
3 celery stalks, chopped
1 medium green pepper, seeds removed and chopped
2 beef bouillon cubes
2 cups warm disinfected water
15oz (425g) can great northern beans

15.25oz (425g) can whole kernel corn
10oz (284g) can Ro-Tel diced tomatoes and green chilies
14.5oz (411g) can diced tomatoes
12.5oz (354g) can diced chicken breast

For the spice blend: (mix these and place them in a plastic bag before you leave home):
1 tsp salt
2½ tsp chili powder
1 tsp onion powder
½ tsp garlic powder

1. Build a medium-flame fire. While the fire is burning down, add the oil to the stew pot.

2. Chop the onion, celery, and green pepper. Add them to the pot.

3. Once the fire has died down and there's a good bed of embers, place the stew pot with the vegetables on the embers.

4. While the vegetables are cooking, combine the beef bouillon cubes and warm water in your water bottle and stir until dissolved.

5. Once the vegetables are soft and brown, add the bouillon broth, great northern beans, and corn to the pot. Give it a stir and allow it to cook long enough that the beans are thoroughly warmed, and then very carefully remove the pot from the fire.

6. Add the Ro-Tel tomatoes and chilies, and the diced tomatoes. Using a spoon (or the camp whisk you made!), stir and mash the mixture. You want to crush the beans as much as possible.

7. Add the diced chicken breast and spice blend, and then place the pot back on the embers. Cook until the chili is thick and hot.

PROJECT:
JOHNNY BREAD

Johnny bread is a campfire staple food made of a mixture of flour and water that creates a thick dough that can be cooked directly on hot embers. It's a simple recipe that may not sound very appetizing, but you'll be amazed at how good it tastes when you're in the outdoors. And it's a ton of fun to make it!

HOW TO MAKE JOHNNY BREAD

Making Johnny bread is super easy and fun. Here's how you do it.

1 Combine equal amounts of all-purpose flour and water in a small container.

2 Using clean fingers or a clean stick, mix the flour and water until a sticky dough begins to form. If the dough is too thin, add a little more flour; if the dough is too thick, add a little more water.

3 Once the ingredients are completely combined, you should have a thick dough ball. Pat the dough ball into a thin cake.

4 Carefully place the cake directly on the embers and cook until one side is done, and then flip the cake over and cook the other side until the cake is cooked. Carefully remove the cake from the embers and enjoy.

COOL TIP!

You can also use ready-to-cook dough options like cinnamon rolls, croissants, or buttermilk biscuits. Simply wrap the uncooked dough around the end of a stick, and slowly cook it over the embers for a delicious treat. When you pull the cooked dough off of the stick, you can fill it with whipped cream, fruit, or even pudding.

PROJECT: COOKING STICK

Cooking food on a stick is one of the simplest and most common methods used in the outdoors. All you need is your knife, a straight and sturdy green wood stick, and a little bushcraft know-how to turn a simple stick into a useful cooking tool. You simply skewer the food and over the fire it goes for a quick meal.

1 Cut a long, straight green wood stick that is about 18 inches (46cm) long and the diameter of your index finger. Make sure the stick is green and not dead. A dead stick will catch fire and break easily, while a green wood stick will be stronger and burn much more slowly.

2 Using your knife, very carefully cut a slit in the end of the stick that is about 2 inches (5cm) long. This will allow you to skewer the food with two points rather than one.

You can make a forked cooking stick by carving the ends of a narrow "V" branch. This stronger option is useful for cooking heavier items, and it's also perfect for roasting up to four marshmallows at once!

3 Using your knife, carve the ends of the stick into two sharp points.

4 Splay the ends of the stick, and then skewer the food onto the stick.

PROJECT: CAMPFIRE TRIPOD

Campfire tripods can be used for lots of things: holding food bags and water pots, hanging pots and pans or gear bags, and even holding up shelters, but what they're best for is cooking over a campfire. A tripod gives you more precise temperature control over a fire because you can open the legs to lower the pot or close them to raise the pot. You can even add a grill top for more cooking options!

1 Gather three straight sticks that are each about the diameter of your thumb and about 5 feet (1.5m) in length.

2 Lay two of the sticks next to each other, and then place the third stick on top of the bottom two to form a pyramid.

3 Place a piece of paracord or thin rope over the sticks about 12 inches (30.5cm) from the top of the sticks. Grasp the two ends of the rope, wrap them around all three sticks, and then secure them with a knot. The knot should *not* be extremely tight.

4 Position the sticks upright, and then twist one stick like the second hand on a clock from the six o'clock position all the way around and back to the six o'clock position to open the legs of the tripod.

5 Tie a bowline knot at one end of a piece of small rope that is about three-quarters the height of the tripod. Affix a toggle on the opposite end of the rope using a clove hitch. Hook the knotted end of the line over the top of the tripod.

6 Feed the toggle through the bale of the pot, and let it hang down.

ADD A GRILL TOP

A tripod can be turned into a grill by adding a wooden grate near the base. To make a grill top, lash green wood support sticks to the three tripod legs about 12 inches (30cm) above the base of the fire pit, and then place green wood sticks across the support sticks. This will enable you to grill vegetables or meat, or even smoke meat over a campfire.

PROJECT: COOKING ROTISSERIE

Have you ever seen those chickens spinning and cooking in a rotisserie oven behind the deli counter? You can do that same thing in the woods, just minus the oven and electricity! Using a cooking rotisserie is the ultimate bushcraft method to cook. It's such a fun and unique way to make a meal.

1 Cut two green wood "Y" branches that are each about 15 inches (38cm) long and about the diameter of your thumb.

2 Insert the "Y" branches into the ground on each side of the fire circle. Make sure the notches of the "Y" branches are about 8 inches from the ground—any higher and the meat will not cook correctly. Also make sure the sticks are inserted deep enough into the ground that they can hold the weight of the food.

MEAT RUB RECIPES

Here are some simple rotisserie ideas that will taste amazing at camp. You'll need to pack the meat in a cooler and over ice. You can make the spice rubs at home (with an adult's help), pack them in resealable plastic bags, and store them in your gear bag. When you're ready to cook, just apply the rubs to the meat after you've skewered it onto the rotisserie.

Beef roast rub: Combine equal parts kosher salt, brown sugar, smoked paprika, granulated raw sugar, garlic powder, black pepper, dry mustard, cumin, and ginger.

Cornish game hen rub: Combine equal parts kosher salt, sugar, onion powder, black pepper, garlic powder, green bell pepper flakes, and paprika.

3 Find two straight green wood sticks that are longer than the width of your campfire. One of the sticks should be about the diameter of your thumb, and the other about the diameter of a pencil. The thicker stick should be about 8 inches (20.5cm) longer than the thinner stick, but both should be long enough to easily fit into the notches of the "Y" branches with room to spare.

4 Lash the thinner stick to the larger stick on one end of the rotisserie, leaving the end of the thicker stick extended about 4 inches (10cm) beyond the end of the thinner stick. (It's important that you do this to allow the rotisserie to be turned.)

COOKING LOW AND SLOW

When you're cooking with a rotisserie over a campfire, it's a method referred to as "low and slow," which means you should keep the flames low and just take your time. You should rotate the meat every few minutes and slowly feed the fire to maintain just enough heat to cook your food thoroughly. On average, a Cornish hen or small beef roast will take about 1 to 1½ hours to cook, but that's okay! Camp cooking should be a fun part of camp life. So relax by the fire, turn the rotisserie occasionally, keep feeding the fire, and just enjoy the outdoors while dinner cooks!

 5 Now that the sticks are lashed, carve sharp points on the sticks at the ends opposite the lashings.

6 On the end of the thicker stick near the lashing, carve three flat areas to create a triangle shape at the point where the stick will fit into the "Y" branch. This will allow you to rotate the meat and cook it evenly. (If you just carve a round end, you won't be able to rotate the meat properly.)

7 Skewer the meat onto the two pointed ends of the straight sticks, and slide it to the center of the sticks. (Using two sticks keeps the meat from spinning freely on the skewer.)

8 Once the meat is centered on the skewer sticks, lash the sharp ends of the sticks together to pinch the meat in place. Secure the skewer in the "Y" branches of the rotisserie.

PROJECT: CRISS-CROSS KITCHEN WITH HOOKS

The criss-cross kitchen is, by far, my favorite type of camp kitchen setup. It can hold numerous pots at varying heights over a campfire. And there are endless options and additions to this system that can make it fit any need. It's great for cooking for larger groups at camp or when cooking with multiple pots over the fire, and it can be easily removed when it's not in use.

1. Cut two green wood "Y" branches that are slightly larger than your thumb in diameter and about 3.5 feet (1m) long.

2. Cut a straight green wood stick that is 1 to 2 feet (30.5cm to 60cm) longer than the width of your campfire and slightly larger than your thumb in diameter.

3. Stick the "Y" branches in the ground at each end of the campfire. (The fork in the "Y" branches should be about 3 feet [1m] above the base of the campfire.) Lay the straight stick across the "Y" branches. (This stick can be removed if not in use to allow total access to the campfire.)

4. Cut two more "Y" branches. (These branches can vary in length, but should be about the diameter of your pinky finger.) Cut them like you would cut wooden tent pegs, with one end of each stick longer than the other end. It's a good idea to make a few sets of hooks in varying lengths.

5 Place the long ends of the "Y" branches back to back, and then use straight lashings to bind them together. Once lashed, the "Y" branches should be a single unit and appear to look like a hanger with a top and bottom hook.

6 Hang one end of the hook over the main cross stick, and then hang the pot on the other end of the hook.

There are numerous ways to make hanging hooks for a criss-cross kitchen. Pictured here are two different styles: the hook on the left is a "Y" branch with a carved notch on the bottom to hold the kettle, while the hook on the right is a "Y" branch attached to the crosspiece with rope. What other hook combinations can you think of? Experiment with different styles and see what you can come up with.

PROJECT: WOODEN GRILL

Grilled food is always a favorite around camp—burgers, steaks, fish, and even sweet corn can all be grilled in the outdoors, but carrying a metal grill grate into camp isn't really practical. Fortunately, a bushcrafter always finds a way to make it work!

1 Gather four green wood "Y" branches that are about 18 inches (46cm) long and about ½ inch (1.5cm) in diameter.

If the grill-top sticks burn up after a few uses, you can simply replace them with new sticks. The frame of the grill, meaning the cross pieces and the "Y" branches, should last much longer and can be stored next to a tree or by the campfire site between trips.

2 Cut approximately 10 straight green wood sticks that are about 15 inches (38cm) long and about ½ inch (1.5cm) in diameter. Make sure you don't choose sticks that are too thick; you want the heat to reach the food.

3 Stick the four "Y" branches in the ground in a square formation around the campfire area to form the frame for the grill grate. The forks of the "Y" branches should be 8 to 10 inches (20.5cm to 25.5cm) from the ground.

4 Position two of the straight sticks between each of the "Y" branches. (At this point, it should look like two parallel bars.)

5 Build a low-flame fire. Once the fire has burned down, place the remaining straight sticks across the grill frame. (It's important to not place the remaining sticks over the fire until it's burned down.)

PROJECT: COOKING SPATULA

A cooking spatula is handy when you're cooking in the outdoors, like when you're cooking scrambled eggs, flipping bacon, and even dishing out sausage gravy and biscuits! When creating this spatula, it's important to keep knife safety in mind. Carving projects like this one can be dangerous because you will be using your knife quite a bit and carving angles, so be very careful and remember the rules for using a knife.

1 Cut a round piece of wood that is about the length and width of the spatula you want to make. Set the piece upright on a sturdy surface, and then place your knife in the center of the wood. Using another piece of wood, strike downward on your knife to wedge it into the wood.

2 Once the knife is wedged into the wood, hit the tip of your knife downward to split the wood. (This is called *batoning*.) When doing this, it's important to not attempt to baton wood that is larger than your knife. Ideally you should only baton wood that is about three-fourths the width of your knife blade.

3 Following the same process, split the wood again, this time removing the rounded outer edge to leave the widest center piece for carving. This center piece should be about ½ inch (1.25cm) thick. Remember that each time you split the wood, you should remove the rounded sides and not the flat sides.

4 Using a piece of charcoal from the campfire, draw the shape of your spatula on a flat side of the wood. Be sure to include a handle and try to make the curves even on both sides.

5 Begin removing material to create the handle by cutting inward and then slowly turning your knife blade toward the top of the handle. Do not cut down toward the bottom of the spatula. Doing so can cause you to cut the grain wrong, and you could end up cutting away the spatula surface.

6 Once you've carved the handle, carve the top and sides, and then carve the front edge into a slant. (The slant will enable you to slide the spatula under things in the pan.)

COOL TIP!

Wood has something called *grain*, which is the direction of the fibers in the wood. Carving against the grain is more difficult than carving along it, but doing so means there is less chance of splitting your piece. Carving along the grain is easier, but it can cause your piece to split. Most carving projects require doing both, so pay attention to how you're cutting and work slowly.

WOOD CARVING IS A SKILL AND A CRAFT

Woodcarvers use specialty tools and techniques to make beautiful works of art. Bushcrafters, however, usually just make useful, utility-type items that will help them accomplish tasks more easily in the woods. Projects like this one are great because they allow you to make both a useful tool and also something that looks cool. It's fun to work on a project like this, so find a nice spot by a stream or sit next to a tree and enjoy the outdoors as you work.

PROJECT: COOKING WHISK

When you're cooking at camp, there are lots of things that need to be mixed: soups, stews, and even eggs. A stick or a fork will work okay, but we are bushcrafters, and we can make a whisk to get the job done better! This is a fun and easy project to complete, and it creates an extremely useful tool to have around the campsite.

1 Find a straight green wood branch that has three to five branches extending out of it. (This might require some looking around, so be patient.)

2 Cut the main branch approximately 6 to 8 inches (15cm to 20.5cm) away from the split where the three to five branches extend out of it.

3 Begin trimming the offshoot branches, starting with the innermost branches. (It's important to cut all the offshoot branches so they're even at the bottom. If you cut some too short, the whisk will be less effective because some branch tips won't reach the bottom of the pan.) Continue trimming until you've removed all the bark on the lower portion of the whisk.

COOL TIP!

This whisk can be made as large or as small as needed. If you're going to use it for an entire camping trip, I recommend removing all the bark from the whisk; it will make it easier to clean after each use. If it's a good, strudy whisk, you'll be able to use it for a long time.

PROJECT: BIRCH BARK DRINKING CUP

This fun project makes a drinking cup using just birch bark and a stick. If you have a community water bucket, everyone can use the bark cup as a water dipper to fill their pots and bottles.

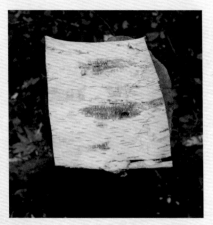

1 Find a birch tree. Using your knife, cut a square section of bark that is about the size of a large book, and then peel the section away from the tree. (If there isn't a birch tree in your area, you will need to do some exploring and experimenting to find a tree with bark that is smooth and flexible when you remove it.) Place the birch bark section on a flat, sturdy surface.

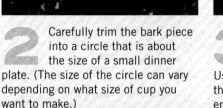 Carefully trim the bark piece into a circle that is about the size of a small dinner plate. (The size of the circle can vary depending on what size of cup you want to make.)

 Find a stick that is about 6 inches (15cm) long and the diameter of your index finger. Using your knife, very carefully round the ends, and then make a split at one end that is about 2 inches (5cm) long.

Grasp the edges of the bark with your fingers placed approximately 2 inches (5cm) apart, and then fold the bark over on itself to create a cone-shaped cup. (Because it will be smoother, use the inside of the bark for the inside of the cup.)

Insert the folded portion of the bark into the split end of the stick.

9

MAINTAINING AND REPAIRING GEAR

Your tools will enable you to make items that provide both comfort and utility at camp. For this reason, it's important to take good care of your tools—axes and knives can become dull, leather and fabrics can become weathered, and tools that go without care can break and become damaged or even unsafe to use. In this chapter, you'll learn some of the basics of caring for your tools as well as how to make some useful items that will make that job easier. Your gear can be your lifeline and keep you safe, so you'll want to treat it with care and respect, and keep it in good working condition.

AXE CARE AND MAINTENANCE

If used correctly and maintained properly, an axe can provide years of service in the woods. Sharpening it regularly, taking care of the handle, and maintaining the leather sheath are all crucial steps for keeping your axe in top working condition.

CARING FOR THE SHEATH

Anything made of leather needs to be conditioned, and that includes your axe sheath; rain, humidity, and heat can all dry it out and cause it to crack. Apply leather conditioner with a soft cloth, or use your fingers to massage it into the leather whenever the leather appears dry or after you've been camping in the rain and snow. (Be sure to allow the sheath to dry at home before applying the conditioner.) If you're using a paste conditioner, massage it into the leather, and then use a blow dryer to warm the leather. This will help the conditioner better saturate the leather. (Later on, you'll learn how to make birch oil, which can be used to condition your sheath.) Also, always make sure the stitching and snaps on the sheath are in good working order. Broken snaps or faulty stitching can mean the blade will be exposed to the elements.

CARING FOR THE HANDLE

If your axe has a wooden handle, the handle will need some care. Boiled linseed oil, which can be purchased at most hardware stores, is an excellent conditioner for a wooden handle. Simply apply a thin coat with a soft, clean cloth, allow it to sit for a few minutes, and then wipe it off with a dry, clean cloth. Be sure to apply oil over the entire handle and also work it into the ends. Over time, the handle will soak up lots of the oil and will eventually become fully conditioned, which will help it last a long time. If you notice that the axe handle has developed cracks or large chips, you may need to replace it. You don't want the axe head flying across camp due to a broken handle!

CARING FOR THE HEAD

The head is the metal part of the axe and should have a light coat of tool oil applied after every camping trip or after use in wet conditions to keep it from rusting. You can find tool oil at most hardware stores; it's inexpensive and works great for keeping your axe head in good condition. Simply use a clean cloth to apply it, and then use a dry, clean cloth to wipe away any excess oil.

SHARPENING THE AXE HEAD

Over time, the sharp cutting edge of the axe head can become dull. Normal axe sharpening should be done after every camping trip or after a few day trips. Here's how to keep the cutting edge sharp.

1 Sit in a comfortable spot, and secure the axe handle underneath your arm with the back of the axe head resting in your nondominant hand. You should be looking down at the sharp edge. Wet your sharpening puck or stone with water (not oil) and then position it against the side of the axe blade so you can still see a gap between the puck and the sharp edge. (Keeping the sharpening stone wet will improve the sharpening process and prevent metal bits from clogging the stone. Also, you should always use water and not oil to wet a sharpening tool. Oil can make a mess, particularly if you've already used oil on the tool and then try to use water.)

2 Slightly tilt the stone into the blade edge until it just comes into slight contact with the edge. (If you go too far, you will grind away the sharp edge of the axe.) Once you have found the point where the stone and the blade's edge just meet, apply medium pressure and begin moving the stone up and down while simultaneously moving it along the length of the axe edge to sharpen it. Make the same number of passes on each side of the sharp edge to ensure the edge is sharpened evenly on both sides.

FILING THE AXE HEAD

If an axe comes into contact with the ground or a rock, it can sometimes become chipped on the sharp edge and will need to be filed. This is uncommon, but here's how to file it in case you do encounter a chip.

1 To file out chips, find a flat, sturdy work area. You'll need a mill bastard file, which is a long, flat file with rough edges on both sides and a flat end. (A mill bastard file is the best type of file to use for filing an axe, but if you want to carry something smaller, a chainsaw file will also work great.)

2 Place the axe head flat on its side, and begin pushing the file forward from the back of the head up to the sharp edge. You should feel the file grinding metal from the axe, and each forward file stroke should cover the full length of the sharp edge of the axe. (It's important to file evenly on both sides. Make the same number of passes on each side of the sharp edge.) Continue on both sides until you've removed the small chips. Once the small chips have been removed, carefully sharpen the edge with a sharpening stone. (Note that if the sharp edge of the axe head is cracked, you should show it to an adult so they can determine if the head needs to be replaced.)

KNIFE CARE AND MAINTENANCE

Your knife is a very important piece of gear—it can be used to cut wood for a shelter, carve shavings to start a campfire, or most importantly, be used to prepare dinner! Because it's such an important bushcraft tool, you need to maintain it so it's always in good working order.

MAINTAINING THE SHEATH AND HANDLE

If your knife has a sheath, check it for rips or broken stitches. (Hey, you're going to learn how to sew in this chapter, so no excuses!) Be sure to oil the sheath if it's leather. You should also inspect the handle of your knife to ensure it's not broken or loose. If it is broken or loose, show it to an adult so they can determine if it needs to be fixed or replaced. A loose knife handle can be dangerous and can result in the knife slipping from your hand.

SHARPENING YOUR KNIFE

Using your knife frequently means it's going to get dull. This is normal and nothing to worry about. Just make sure you do not keep using it when it seems to be getting dull; using a dull knife can be dangerous. Using a sharp knife is actually much safer and reduces the chances of injury.

Sharpening your knife is very similar to how you sharpen your axe. Here's how you do it.

COOL TIP!

Try to sharpen your knife every night after a long day in the outdoors. This is something most experienced bushcrafters will do at camp.

1 Sit in a comfortable area, and hold your knife so you are looking down at the sharp edge of the blade and the sharp tip is pointed away from you.

2 Place a sharpening stone or puck flat against the side of the knife. At this point, you should see a slight gap between the stone and the sharp edge of the knife.

3 Slowly tilt the stone into the blade edge just until it comes into slight contact with the sharp edge. (If you tilt it too far, you will grind off the sharp edge.) Once you find where the stone and sharp edge meet, use medium pressure to very carefully begin moving the stone up and down against the sharp edge while simultaneously moving the stone along the length of the sharp edge.

4 Once one side is sharpened, carefully reverse the position of the knife in your hand so the tip of the blade is pointing toward you. Continue the process on the other side of the sharp edge, making sure to sharpen both sides equally by making the same number of passes on each side.

KEEP IT
SAFE
Be extremely careful when sharpening a knife or an axe. Your fingertips can be cut very easily, so work slowly.

STROPPING FOR A SUPER-SHARP EDGE

Once you've sharpened your knife with a sharpening stone, you can use something called a *strop* to get your knife super sharp! A strop is a piece of leather, sometimes with a buffing compound applied to it, that enables you to put a super-fine, super-sharp edge on your knife. Stropping your knife blade is a good addition to sharpening, but you'll need to strop often if you're using your knife regularly because you can't use a strop to make a dull knife sharp again—only a sharpening stone can be used to do that. Stropping just adds an extra-sharp edge to an already sharp blade.

To strop a knife blade, place the sharp edge of the blade as flat as possible against the surface of the strop. (Only the sharp edge should be touching the strop.) Pull the knife blade *toward* you as you simultaneously slide the blade from the sharp point to the handle end. Repeat the process several times, and then place the knife in your opposite hand and repeat on the other side an equal number of times to ensure you strop the blade evenly.

Note that when you strop, it's important *not* to roll the sharp edge of the blade up onto the leather or to *push* the sharp edge into the leather surface. Doing so can make the knife edge dull and also cut the strop.

SEWING TO REPAIR GEAR

Sewing may seem unrelated to bushcraft, but it's actually a very important skill for every bushcrafter to know. Many of the items you will carry as a bushcrafter have been made using some type of sewing—your axe sheath, gloves, and even your backpack all required sewing when they were manufactured, so sometimes these items also require sewing to repair. Sewing also enables you to make unique items for use in the woods. Once you learn how to sew, you will be able to fix all kinds of things.

ESSENTIAL SEWING SUPPLIES AND BASIC SEWING STITCHES

Sewing requires some supplies, so it's a good idea to keep a small sewing kit in your backpack for those on-the-go repairs or even for projects you want to create. Here are some must-have sewing supplies.

Needles

"S" needle This will be the most-used needle in your sewing arsenal. It has an "S" shape and a very sharp point with three sides. This needle is extremely strong, and the shape, unlike a straight needle, will enable you to push hard on the needle when you're working with stronger materials. This needle can penetrate thick leather, heavy fabrics, and even tree bark with ease.

Glovers needle This needle is great for sewing through thin leather or punching holes in leather or other materials. The point is three-sided and the sides are sharp, which helps the needle cut through thicker, tougher materials.

Point needle This needle style is what you typically think of when you think of a sewing needle—it's long and straight, with a sharp point. This style works great for stitching woven cloth fabrics such as cotton or wool because it can easily slide through the weave of the material without cutting it.

"S" needle

Glovers needle

Point needle

Threads

Thread is what holds everything together. It comes in different colors and sizes, and is made of different materials, but it all serves the same purpose. Bushcrafters generally only use two to three types of threads: artificial sinue, bonded polyester, and cotton.

Artificial sinue
This waxed polyester thread is very traditional looking and has a super-high breaking strength. It's ideal for repairing leather and stitching heavy-duty materials like bark.

Cotton thread
This is the least-used thread in the outdoors because it's the weakest, but that doesn't mean it isn't useful. If your pants get ripped or you get a hole in your favorite winter hat, you can use this thread to repair these lighter items with ease.

Bonded polyester thread
This heavy-duty thread is generally used to sew thick fabrics together. Knife sheaths are often sewn with this type of thread and can be repaired with it as well. It's also great for repairing items that require stronger mending, like backpacks, tarps, outerwear, and hiking boots.

THREADING A NEEDLE

Before you stitch anything, you need to know how to thread a needle. To do so, cut the end of the thread so it's not frayed, and then insert the cut end into the eye of the needle. (If the thread seems too tight in the eye, use a larger needle.) Pull approximately 8 inches (20.5cm) of thread through the eye, and then let the loose end hang as you sew. (Do not knot the thread.)

Performing a Saddle Stitch

The saddle stitch is very strong and is used mainly in leatherwork, but can also be used for heavy fabrics, tents, tarps, and packs.

1 Insert the needle from the front, and then pull it through to the back. Next, insert it into the back, and then pull it back through to the front. Continue until you reach the end of the area you are sewing.

2 Working backward, insert the needle into the original holes, and then pull it back through completely to close each stitch.

3 Continue until you're back to the original starting point, but don't close the last stitch.

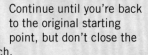

4 Using a simple knot, close the last stitch.

Performing a Running Stitch

The running stitch is often used when making camp bedding or sewing items that will later require the thread to be removed. This is a lighter-strength stitch.

1 Beginning on one end, insert the needle from the front and then pull it through to the back.

2 Insert the needle into the back and then pull it through to the front. Continue until you reach the end of the area you are sewing.

3 When you reach the end of the fabric, pull the needle part way through, leaving the loose end on the opposite side.

4 Thread the loose end through the loop, and then tie the ends off into a simple knot to close the stitch.

Performing a Whip Stitch

The whip stitch is used to bind the edges of two pieces of material. This stitch is fast and easy to sew, and has medium binding strength.

1 Loop the needle through the fabric and then tie the ends into a simple knot to secure the thread.

2 Insert the needle through the top of the fabric, loop it around the outer edge and back to the front. Repeat at an angle.

3 When you reach the end of the fabric, pull the needle part way through, leaving the loose end on the opposite side.

4 Thread the loose end through the loop and then tie the ends off into a simple knot to close the stitch.

PROJECT: BIRCH OIL

Oil is a very important component for caring for your bushcraft tools. Metal components such as knife blades and axe blades can rust if they get wet and are not dried properly. And leather and wood components can dry out, crack, or break apart if they aren't properly lubricated. For these reasons, many bushcrafters always carry a small container of tool oil in their packs, but you can also render a very useful oil from the bark of the birch tree. That's right! This incredibly versatile oil is flammable and water-resistant, which means you can use it on your tools, use it to treat your leather goods, use it as a fire starter, and even use it to repel bugs! Making birch oil is one of my favorite bushcraft projects.

FUN FACT!

Even though bushcrafters call it "oil," birch oil is actually a mixture of birch oil and birch tar. The combination of the two ingredients is commonly referred to as "birch oil" by bushcrafters.

HOW TO MAKE BIRCH OIL

This is a super-fun project! You'll need one small metal container and one large metal container with a tight-fitting lid. (Stainless steel containers will work best.) You'll also need some fire-resistant gloves—fireplace gloves work really well and will keep your hands protected.

1 Punch a hole about the diameter of a pencil in the lid of the larger container. Fill the larger container to the very top with broken-up birch bark, and then secure the lid on the container.

2 Dig a hole in the ground where you are going to start the campfire. The hole should be deep enough that it can hold both containers securely once dirt is piled around the containers, but not so deep that both containers will be covered. Place the smaller container in the bottom of the fire hole with the open end facing up.

3 Place the larger container upside down on top of the smaller container, making sure the hole in the lid of the larger container is positioned directly over the smaller container. (This hole is how the birch oil will drain into the smaller container.)

4 Pack dirt into the hole around the smaller container. Pack enough dirt around the larger container that about one-third of the larger container is covered with dirt and both containers are held securely in place.

FUN FACT!

Birch oil has a very unique smell. Some people like the smell, while others do not, but it does help repel bugs, and it also gives wood and leather a very rich, classic look. If you put birch oil on a new axe handle, it will make it look like an antique from the frontier. That's cool!

5 Build a fire over the containers. As the bark heats up, it will begin rendering the oil into the smaller container. It may take several hours to complete the process, so be sure to keep the fire going, and be careful not to knock over the containers when adding wood to the fire.

6 Once the process is completed, use a stick to move all the hot embers as far away from the containers as possible, and allow the containers to cool completely. Once cool, put on the fire-resistant gloves, and place one hand on top of the larger container. Apply light pressure to keep the smaller container covered, and then carefully dig out the dirt around the containers. Once the dirt has been cleared, remove the top container. You should now see a black liquid in the smaller container. That is birch oil!

7 Transfer the birch oil to a resealable metal or plastic container, and place it in your backpack for future use.

PROJECT: PINE-GLUE STICK

Another cool bushcraft project is making a pine-glue stick. Pine glue was traditionally used by Native Americans to secure arrowheads onto arrows, but it can be used for lots of different things in the woods. I've used it for making baskets, patching holes in my favorite pair of boots, and even as a fire extender.

1 Gather equal amounts of the following materials: pine sap, charcoal, and a binding material such as dried grass or cattail fluff. You'll also need a short stick and a small metal dish or container.

2 Place the pine sap in the metal dish, crush the charcoal into a fine powder, and shred the cattail fluff or finely shred the grass.

3 Place the container near, but not in the fire. You want to slowly heat the pine sap until it's just melted. If you heat it too quickly, it can catch fire.

4 Once the sap is melted, use the stick to pick out any large chunks of dirt, rock, or bark. Combine equal parts sap, charcoal powder, and binding material in the dish, and then use the stick to stir the ingredients together.

5 Once the mixture begins to cool, shape it onto the stick. It should form a glob that can then be molded like clay before it dries. Now you have a pine-glue stick! To use the stick, warm the glob over a campfire, and then apply it to wherever the glue is needed.

COOL TIP!

If the final mixture isn't firm enough to be molded, reheat it in the fire and then add more charcoal. If the mixture is too dry and appears to be cracking, reheat it in the fire and then add more binding material.

INDEX

To my grandfather—the hikes down to the railroad tracks and the summer mornings fishing at Tuscarora all molded my life forever.

ACKNOWLEDGMENTS

My wife, Brooke, who reviews all my writing and has always been there for me, and now fills the role my teachers once filled as I was growing up. She's always telling me I can do more and to pursue my dreams, even when she's reminding me that I'm not good at spelling and that I write in 47 different tenses. (That's why I keep her around.) Also, my parents, Susan and Dan, who 99 percent of the time probably think they raised a maniac, but they've always been there for me. Everything and everyone you cross paths with in life leads you to where you are now—good and bad, happy and sad. I would like to thank everyone for their help over the years! It has truly led me to this moment in time.

ABOUT THE AUTHOR

Dan Wowak was born and raised in Mahanoy City, Pennsylvania, a small coal-mining town in the heart of the Appalachian Mountains. During his childhood, Dan spent much of his time in the woods exploring, hiking, camping, and fishing. After college, Dan worked in the juvenile justice field for nearly a decade, and during that time used the outdoors as an escape, often using his time off to explore the outdoors and train himself on different outdoor skills. He found extreme pleasure in the pain of outdoor life and welcomed the challenges and hardships Mother Nature threw at him. In late 2016, the company Dan worked for closed, leaving him without a job and also a lack of desire to work in the justice field any longer. Looking to do something better with his life led him to one of the most challenging events of his life: participating in The History Channel's *Alone Season 3* series, where he was sent into the mountains of Patagonia to live alone. He survived for 51 days while only eating nine fish, but the experience changed Dan's life. After finishing the show, he began working on building an outdoor brand so he could share his knowledge and passion for the outdoors through training and products. In 2017, Dan officially started Coalcracker Bushcraft and the Appalachian Bushman School. Over the next few years, Coalcracker Bushcraft grew to be one of the top bushcraft retailers in the country, and the Appalachian Bushman School trained hundreds of students in the art of outdoor living. Since then, Dan has become a YouTube personality known for his short, to-the-point outdoor tutorials. Dan continues to grow Coalcracker Bushcraft by designing new and innovative outdoor products and also teaching new bushcrafters through the Appalachian Bushman School. He works with several outdoor companies to bring bushcraft skills to others and to expose more people to his life passion.